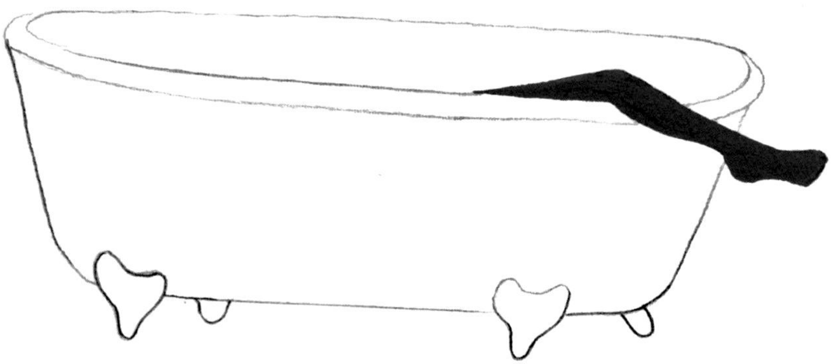

Tub by Anju Gaston

The Mays Anthology XXVI

Edited by Eimear Ní Chathail
and Elizabeth Howcroft

Guest Edited by Alexandra Shulman

VARSITY

Varsity Publications Ltd
16 Mill Lane
Cambridge CB2 3RF

First published 2018 by Varsity Publications Ltd

Varsity Business Manager – Mark Curtis business@varsity.cam.ac.uk

ISBN Number 978-0-902240-49-0

Designed and typeset by Biddles Books

Cover Design by Alisa Santikarn

Printed and bound by Biddles Books Limited, King's Lynn, Norfolk

British Library Cataloguing in Publication Data:

A CIP catalogue record of this book is available from the British Library.

Further copies of this book any other titles in the series can be bought through most booksellers or direct from Varsity Publications at the address above or at:

www.varsity.co.uk/themays

www.themaysanthology.co.uk

Acknowledgements:

We would like to offer our very special thanks to Dr. Franklin and Mark Curtis for their constant assistance and encouragement in bringing this project to fruition. *The Mays Anthology* depends on them, and on the Varsity board, for its yearly publication, and it is due to them that this book has been published.

We are also incredibly grateful and deeply indebted to the following for their financial support:

Churchill College, Cambridge
Emmanuel College, Cambridge
Gonville and Caius College, Cambridge
Jesus College, Cambridge
Lucy Cavendish College, Cambridge
Magdalene College, Cambridge
Newnham College, Cambridge
Queens' College, Cambridge
Sidney Sussex College, Cambridge
Trinity College, Cambridge
Trinity Hall, Cambridge
All Souls College, Oxford
Christ Church, Oxford
Exeter College, Oxford
Jesus College, Oxford
Merton College, Oxford
New College, Oxford
and
The Times Literary Supplement

Editors: Elizabeth Howcroft and Eimear Ní Chathail

Oxford Associate Editor: Katie Dent

Deputies to Oxford Associate Editor: Victoria Gawlik and Daniel Haynes

Assistant Curator: Leah Wild

Design and Production: Ryan Wightman

Events: Livia Fries

Publicity: Anna Hollingsworth

Treasurer and Deputy Publicity: Sam Ashbridge

Social Media: Sophie Zhang

Submissions Officer: Isabelle Burroughes

Poetry Selection Subcommittee:

Edwin Boadu
Jonathan Chan
Ellamae Lepper
Michael Tigchelaar
Matthew Wilson

Prose Selection Subcommittee:

Sana Khan
Marcus McCabe
Naoise Murphy
Caithlin Ng

Artwork Selection Subcommittee:

Elizabeth Huang
Leah Wild
Ryan Wightman

Contents

Drawing (of) St Jerome by Elaine Robertson

Foreword

There's the whole world out there and every time we write a story, an article, a poem, or paint a picture and take a photograph we are making a part of it our own. That is what this anthology is about.

The opportunity and ability to take the stuff of our lives and mould it into the shape that we choose is a privilege. To be able to showcase that creation to others even more so. We all have our memories, our experiences, the everyday of our existence but only some of us are able to take this matter and turn it into another form – of printed words or images.

Storytelling is one of the universals. The desire to share information about the world in which we exist, is something that has been part of mankind since our earliest days. From the Lascaux cave paintings to the messages of the touring minstrel and onto the myriad opportunities for creativity today, the methods might change but the core of what we do remains the same. We turn thoughts into words and pictures.

Throughout my life, outside of what might be termed my "job" I have always tried to achieve some private work of this kind, firstly via poetry – unlike the poets contained in these pages mine was never published – then through photography, fiction and non-fiction writing. I suspect, like many who have contributed to this volume, I have pressed delete, delete, drunk more coffee than is wise, felt that hit of joy when I know a sentence has struck the perfect curve, got lost in the gap between what I want to say and what I am saying, and doubted that I have anything worth saying anyway.

As can been seen in this volume's content, there is so often though, something worth saying about the most ordinary of moments, the details becoming the big picture: A row of artichokes, a hangover, a typewriter ribbon, the blue of a Finnish sky. Writing here, now at a kitchen table with a noisy wasp hopelessly crashing itself against a pane of glass next to a wide open garden door, there are so many things I could say, and so few that I will.

Creative writing offers great freedom but the greatest skill is surely in the edit – the decision of what to bin, the darlings to be murdered, the clever ideas that obfuscate rather than add. And the same applies to visual art.

Given that world of material we have at our fingertips, how do we chose what part of it to claim our own and then what do we do with it? That is the biggest challenge, but when we succeed, on our own terms, it is exhilarating. I hope all of the fresh talents showcased in the following pages, are feeling and will continue to feel that way.

Alexandra Shulman

A Row of Artichokes to Keep the Spirits Away

Omer Friedlander

I had only realized later that I had planted rows of massive artichoke plants along the perimeter of the property, in order to keep the spirits away, because of my grandmother. The artichokes would nod their spruce-cone heads at me before I turned the light off and I was comforted by the phalanx of green guardians. It was my grandmother, Savta Rivka, who told me about the artichokes. She would lie on her bed covered in blankets and patterned rugs, which made her look like a mummified queen in her sarcophagus cocoon, while thousands of moths fluttered around her in search of a light source. I would lie beside her every night, listening for a pulse. Sometimes, I would hear her pulse and her stories, whose words beat with the same steady rhythm of roots travelling through thick soil. On our best plate, which was blue-rimmed, we laid down offerings for her: dried dates stuffed with almonds, sweet, dripping peaches, and clusters of sour grapes which were the colour of her eyes. She told me that there was a high concentration of spirits in the dust of the limestone walls surrounding our house and in unwashed plates. 'The trick is to have a garden. That way you can feed your family and keep the spirits out. Try planting artichokes, we haven't had artichokes in a while, ever since your mother started buying asparagus instead.'

After my grandfather, Saba Shmuel, died she refused to leave her room entirely and stayed there for the next twenty years, outliving her husband yet refusing to live without him. I was the one who found them both. Saba Shmuel had died standing up, the way he used to write and read for hours every day in his study at his wooden lectern. When he was still alive, I would sneak into his study to look his wallpaper which was made up of rows and rows of bright beetles, at the yellowed elephant tusks hanging like pirate scimitars, the giant turtle shells shining like shields, the human spine, the crocodile skin, the octopus tentacles in glowing jars and the fully stocked liquor cabinet with Japanese whiskeys, Turkish arak, and Greek ouzo.

Savta Rivka had died in her room of course, but strangely this was the first time I had seen the blue-rimmed plate of offering empty. The peach pits lay around her bed like tiny moon craters. Grape stems seemed to grow out of her hair, fitting her with a twisted crown.

Every time I heard the spirits, I would plant another artichoke. My garden has become so full of them that I could hardly step outside and it made me think of Savta Rivka who had stayed in her room. Once the ground was entirely covered I watered the artichokes through the open window using a hose. I kept the windows open, even though it was cold, and their stems grew at an angle as they stretched their necks towards the inside of the house. I made sure the artichokes stayed mostly intact by eating the leaves off of a different head each day. I planted the artichokes to keep the spirits away – like Savta Rivka, who had grown sick of asparagus, had taught me.

Senate House by Matthew Seccombe

Narcoleptic

Paul Norris

Ah! vous dirai-je, maman,
ce qui cause mon tourment ?

it met you • like a faint
hills murmur • their rolling song
don't argue • wear your station

on a placard • you wake in
the right place • you're tired everywhere
and you tried • everything but

you arrived • before it made sense
the dream foils • your eyelids
search for darkness • brittle stars crinkle

spots as pearls • spotless
in winter • the hills are white
your dreaming • changes voice

you were dreamed • taken
past a sentence • no subject
dream seeking • a dreamer

fill the glass • you've had enough
bottled up • she promises
consolation • beyond bars

days are long • her white dress
surrounds her • like an iris
you remember • not to wake

広島[1]

Theo Akiyama

when air turned jelly
moves like a block
mountains wobble
watches stop

flash cloud bombs out
sky cataract
blooms

she
turns
to
the
sun
with
white
peonies
on
her
dress
on
the
hospital
bed

says nothing but
points at her eyebrows.

1 In 2013 I visited my Japanese grandmother in Hiroshima (広島), her hometown. It was the first time we had made contact since she held me as a baby. She was 94 years old.

Mahogany Clam

Crystal Liu

The lake is cold, the diver
like a gloved hand on its back.
    Deep in Norwegian waters
three hundred meters inside the Arctic
circle, he mines for palm-heavy
plums, coaxes closed bodies
from the sand.
    He says they live to be four hundred
years old. That they taste of sweet ocean umami.
I watch him take out his knife,
the swift scoop of the blade –
    This is another sort of love,
        pearl-less and ancient.
The rise and fall of its ragged gasps.
The fleshy thing glistening in the wild air.

Eros on the Seine

Harri Adams

儚く過ぎて行く日々の中で…
Utada Hikaru, 'Beautiful World'

Bass drums: shelling – for the moment (not blown to filings)
File's still, circles them: the jumping-at-bullet-thumping
Pair – snares hailing at their feet – in their bloodstreams – rapture.

Frills fly bloody as when, surging, the wind in Autumn
Swings trees' skirts in a flamenco, and scatters leaves like
Wyrm's breath; sparks onto your collar up close – *Attention!*

Gold shells scratching at your fingers – it takes so little –
Do or die, or would you do and then die? Enraptured:
They're both blameless, her especially, shameless, meet the

Beat time's beating on their breasts with a *faire la bise*, and
Hot red blossoms in their skin, in this thunderflash's
Burst – black flowers? But then, who'd want to live to eighty?

Play safe? Streetlamps as grenades – there's no gain – the circle
Breaks –
                would you cross to the bank, join the fray there?

Hour Glass Loves on Moon Spun Nights by Sophie Hardcastle

Easkey Bay

Will Maclean

Document coast.
 Basalt or else.
Sea is supposed
 To hold isles.
Written gulls call
 Tracing in fall
Dipped nimbus weight
 In sky's green miles.
Taut water moves
 Proving still. Sound.
Terns touch ground, e
 Rupt, shoot off, ask
What names they found.
 The more you look
The more I look
And colour blooms:
Grey pearl pink slate
 1 2 3 4.
And yet you look
 Too much like me.
You look too much.
 How the sea looks,
How the air hopes
 And brushes, its
Hopeful rushes
 Of wind, and its
Way of rippling,
 And further still
How the figured
 Teetering of
Bars printed out
 Onto the wan

Atlantic scar
 Ring, from afar
Forging circles
 And how greens haze.
Coast documents
In lines what is
Land, Irish, and
 Comes counting, one
Two flee four five
 A haon a dó.
Coastal text time.

 No time next time.
And it's this, this
 Being held, that makes
Saprophytic
 Gleams on emblem
Shoreline seems death's
 Country, homeland.
Distance again.
 I feel a pen
And the weight of
 Of your lyric
Hand. Now is when
 I take this sand
For homeness then.

Printshop Drawing #1, #2, and #3 by Charlotte Clark

Eleanor Myerson

Clarity

Here's a question – when couples say 'to have and to hold', who's having and who's holding?

She was standing in the kitchen, Clementine, by the stacked plates in the sink. Her hair was curling onto her forehead, and she was smiling – no, she was laughing to herself – no, she was smiling at Lara. Lara couldn't believe how beautiful she looked. Clementine, shaking out the dough with her bare hands, her lashes over her cheeks with the flour from the dough shaking onto her shirt. The stove scattered with basil leaves and stalks. The light in the kitchen was too harsh, synthetic, but on Clementine's face it fell so softly. Lara could hardly stand to watch. The elegance of Clementine with her thin fingers in the crust, flicking her wrists so the dough stretched to an oval in the air. Lara thought, that's a gesture that could make a person fall in love.

In amongst this gesture, Clementine found space to say – 'Shake it out.' Somehow, she told Lara – 'I can't follow recipes.' When Lara looked back on it later, holding it in her mind, she couldn't place Clementine's speech into her picture. She heard the voice echoing, but all she saw was the smile, and laughter, and flour dusting the spotted silk shirt. Lara looked at her hands. Clementine slid the dough into the oven and came back to the table. Lara could have reached out and touched her, but she didn't.

Clementine's eyelids shone. From time to time she played with the hoops hanging from her ears. She tilted her head. She rested her cheek on her hand.

'Shall I put the second one in?'

Lara hesitated.

"I'm not that hungry," Clementine went on. 'So I probably won't, but if you want I will.'

Lara can't remember what she told her. Did they eat both pizzas? She knows that Clementine kept apologizing about the dough. 'I'm not good at cooking.'

'Don't apologize,' Lara kept saying. 'It's nice!'

'You're good at cooking,' Clementine said. 'And you were so calm about it.'

'Oh, well,' Lara said. 'I did a lot of cooking when I was living at home.'

She had actually been disappointed with the meal she had cooked for Clementine the week before. The rice had been sticky, and she preferred the dish with cauliflower not squash. But she was glad Clementine had liked it.

'I got so distracted when I was cooking,' Clementine said. 'I kept stopping to use the dough for my art!'

The table was pushed into the corner of the room, and her laptop sat between them while she chose music. But the shared account was being used from elsewhere, and when she had chosen a song, she couldn't play it. The flat joined onto no other wall at this side. The window faced out onto a dark courtyard. Still.

'Oh, I know,' Clementine said. 'Do you want to watch the videos I made earlier?'

'Videos?'

'With the dough...' Clementine searched for them. 'When I was making the pizza.'

Lara widened her eyes. 'Oh!' She watched Clementine opening the clips. She had pictured sculptures – but Clementine had stretched the dough into a frame, and inserted the film she'd shot inside it. Lara wished she had an intelligent response. 'It's great,' she said.

'Really?'

'Really. I love it.'

Clementine tapped on her laptop keyboard as they talked. The plates had been cleared from the table. Lara unwrapped the desserts she had brought, and Clementine fetched spoons. But the jars sat uneaten while they went on talking – it was an hour before they remembered about the desserts. When they did, Clementine was surprised by the gold frosting over the top of the chocolate. 'This looks so good!' she said. Lara was relieved. She'd had trouble deciding what to bring, not feeling like drinking, but struggling to think of a better object to bring than a bottle of wine. She looked at Clementine holding the spoon in her fingers, and held her breath. The tip of her nose, the dappled colour of her eyes.

Clementine fiddled with her mug as Lara followed her expression shifting, her mouth. Lara thought, I've told her more about myself than I told my ex in two and half years. Then she reflected, and admitted, well, no – but that's the sort of generalization a person might make if they were falling in love.

The scene lent its glow to the clutter on the shelves, the torn posters on the walls.

'Masculinity is about absence,' Clementine was saying.

'Yeah,' Lara said.

'If you like someone, why wouldn't you go out with them?' Clementine was saying.

'Definitely.' Lara touched her chin.

'I don't know about marriage,' Clementine was saying.

'Me either...' Lara laughed.

'What?'

'Oh, nothing...'

It was growing late. 'Have you ever had a tarot reading?' Lara was saying.

'No! Have you?'

Lara hesitated, not knowing why she had brought that up. She'd had her tarot read by a woman she dated over the summer. 'Yeah,' she said, furrowing her brow. 'Anyway-'

There was silence in the kitchen. Lara half reached for Clementine's hand. She looked down.

'I feel shy,' Clementine said.

'Me too,' said Lara. It was true, the words stuck in her throat. She took off her glasses. The women drew their chairs closer together, and Lara put her hand on the back of her neck. They kissed. She put her hand on Clementine's shoulder. Clementine's hand was in Lara's short hair.

'Shall we go into my room?' Clementine said.

The first time they had kissed was on a street corner. The damp pavement reflected back the moon.

'My mouth is so dry,' Clementine had said. 'I can't!'

She had kissed Lara's neck instead. Lara kissed her cheek. They held hands.

The second time they had kissed was in Lara's hallway, hushing each other in case her housemates walked in. The floorboards creaked.

'Do you want me to go?' Clementine had said.

'No...' Lara had said. 'But I have class in the morning...'

'I'll go,' Clementine said. Then – oh... Lara had thought. This is how it's supposed to be. She had held Clementine to her, and Clementine held her back. Clementine tugged gently on the back of her dress. She bit softly at Lara's neck. When they kissed their teeth clashed slightly. Lara felt like she was melting.

'Okay,' Clementine had whispered. 'Bye!'

Her head tilted in the doorway as she left, her eyes bright. When she was gone Lara looked at her phone to check the time. Any amount of time could have passed, she had thought. It had been about fifteen minutes.

Now they were kissing again. 'I hate the light in my room,' Clementine was saying. She was right: it was institutional. She turned it off and the room was pitch black.

'I'll get the lamp from the kitchen,' she said.

They sat on the bed in the light from the lamp. Lara touched her arm. And then –

It is tempting to write what happened next, but not possible. I have been the person reading endless prose about erections and the joy that it is to be a man who can make a girl come, and this is a missed opportunity, in a way, to add my side. But I have no solution to the problem of the boys. Yes, you, the marvellous allies, sharing online links as I type; yes, even you who, if I asked straight readers to skip ahead, might obey. It's too much of a risk, when it was never meant for you, for him. I'm sorry.

Lara and Clementine lay back in the sheets.

'I should go to sleep,' Clementine said. 'I have a supervision in the morning. You can stay, if you want.'

'I'll stay,' she said. 'Can I borrow your makeup remover?'

'It's in the bathroom.'

Lara cleaned her face and washed her hands. She looked at herself in the mirror, the shadows under her eyes. She turned off the light in the kitchen as she passed. She kissed Clementine's shoulder as she was falling asleep.

'What's the time?' Clementine said, waking up.

It was the middle of the night.

'Oh...I thought it was morning,' she said. She rested her head on Lara's chest.

'What's the time?' Lara thought. She could hear voices on the street outside.

It was seven o' clock. She felt wide-awake. She looked at Clementine huddled in the pillows. She went to fetch water from the sink.

'Hey,' Lara whispered. Clementine slept. 'Hey,' she said softly, touching her shoulder.

'Oh!' Clementine started.

'Hey,' Lara said softly. 'I'm sorry – I should go soon. I wanted to say...'

'Oh...'

Clementine nestled into Lara's arms. 'I had a dream my teeth were falling out,' she said.

'It's quite common,' Lara said, putting her cheek next to her hair.

'Yeah...'

Lara had to leave. But when Clementine kissed her she held her in her arms. It didn't matter how long she had – again, she had the feeling that she was outside time.

In the end, 'I should go,' Lara said.

Clementine slipped on a t-shirt. 'Do you mind if I let you out the back?' she said. 'Otherwise I'll have to go and unlock the gates.'

'That's fine.'

They went together into the other room. Clementine laughed. 'You'll have to climb out of the window,' she said. 'I'm sorry, this is really peak.'

Lara laughed too. 'It's fine.'

Clementine pushed up the window, and Lara climbed onto the sill. They looked at each other and smiled.

'Will you hand me out my things?' Lara said.

I am aware where the story should finish. With Lara and Clementine sitting at a corner table in a cafe.

'I just can't,' Clementine was saying. 'I'm sorry – I really like you, I just can't.'

And Lara replying, as if with another's voice, 'It's fine, really. This can't be something else for you to worry about. You've got enough to deal with. If you're worrying, that makes the decision for you.' She looked across at Clementine's tired eyes, looking sad and beautiful above someone else's sweater.

But I hate to write a sad story about gay women. So, instead of Lara on her bench alone, I'll end this here, with her climbing out of Clementine's window on a wintry Monday morning. Then at least in structure, if not theme, I can call this comedy.

'Oh,' said Clementine. 'The gate's already open.'

Builders were coming through the gate. One stood at the entrance, propping it open. Lara looked out and laughed. It was just a short drop. She hooked her leg over the sill. One man looked up, saw the woman in the inside-out dress sitting on the windowsill, and the woman in the t-shirt and rumpled curling hair standing laughing inside the room. Lara hooked her other leg over and jumped. She held her hands out for her bag. Clementine dangled it down for her to catch.

'Bye,' Clementine said, putting her hand to her mouth.

'Bye,' Lara said, smiling.

The builders stood to one side to let her pass into the street. The day had already begun. The commuters were on their way to the train station. She pulled her coat around her, staring at the people on the street as if through a pane of glass. None of them had held Clementine in their arms minutes before. When she breathed out, she was amazed to find the air turned white as always, and the passersby hardly noticed her. She would have thought there would be more obvious signs of change. Shaking her head, she crossed her arms and walked on over the bridge, where the water on the river was strewn with fallen leaves. If every week could begin like this, she thought, I'd be alright.

Thumbs

Lev Crofts

His eyes unstuck into the white light of a sterile room. The sleep that had built up between his eyelids peeled away like a wax strip, and the pain began to spin his cognition. The last thing he remembered was a bumble, a Wodehousian pirouette over the family dog leading to a luge down the stairs. It must have been painful – and embarrassing – he was sure, but noting that he was, in fact, still alive had rephrased his accident from a tragedy into a comedy. *What a way to go*, he thought, chuckling, *one step away from slipping on a banana peel and flailing to my death into a sword juggler. Well, no Darwin Award for today, I suppose, but maybe if I'm lucky I could still filch £250 from You've Been Framed…*

Just as he crashed his train of thought, the door swung open and an unpleasantly cheerful young doctor came into the room, hands in his pockets with the thumbs sticking out, smiling like a monkey on morphine.

'How are we today then?' He said, picking up the clipboard hanging at the end of the man's bed, 'looks like we took a bit of a tumble.'

I took a bit of a tumble, and I am as well as can be expected. There is no we – unless I have been through matrimony while I slept, we are not a couple, he snapped back wittily, though – of course – purely fictionally for the audience of his own monologue.

'Yeah okay, mostly just my pride that's bruised, I reckon.'

As the doctor nodded and smiled politely, the man's eyes slowly fixed upon the medic's hands. They were *bizarre*. The thumbs that had neatly sidled out of his pockets were protruding downwards from a second set of thumbs – albeit in the normal place followed by the usual four fingers. The doctor raised his head to make eye-contact, and the man immediately flashed his gaze back to the bedsheet overlaying him. *What a rude moment of weakness*, he chided himself, *never stare. Poor man, some people are born differently, you know, the things he must have been through! What a horrible childhood it must have given him, children can be so cruel, can't they?* The doctor asked a few routine questions as the man strained to keep his gaze above his nose. After assuring the man that – once a nurse came to perform cursory knee knocks and extract the necessary fluids – he would be able to leave, the quadro-thumbed physician made his exit.

Would those make you better or worse at video games? He ruminated, tucked tightly into his bed with the blanket tickling his chin. *Gloves! God, that man must have a hard time buying gloves. You'd buy the regular kind and then cut holes, I suppose.* To his relief, his thoughts were soon interrupted with a plate of limp food. He wrestled his arms out of the army-tucked bed, and screamed at the sight he saw. Two fleshy spatulas sat at the end of his arms: no more than four fingers stretching from each palm, with no right angles in sight.

'My thumbs!' He yelled. 'The bastard's taken my thumbs!'

As he began flailing and screaming, the nurse, calmly and professionally, reached for her walkie-talkie and raised it to her lips.

'Dr. Pollocks, we have another complaint.'

Ten minutes later, the doctor swaggered into the room – this time leaving behind his cheer. The man lunged at him as soon as his eyes caught the white-coat, pinning him to the door by his lapels. The words 'bastard' and 'thumbs', smattered with a few articles of possession, were the only things audible through the white-noise of his ramblings. He made several attempts to pull at Pollocks's newly-ordained digits, but the removal of a key-player from his instinctual grasping mechanism turned them into nothing more than aggressive low-fives.

'Sir, *please*, calm down, this can all be explained,' Dr. Pollocks assured him, calmly sitting the muttering man onto the bed. For the first time since his discovery, the man accepted silence.

'Your chart says you're an organ donor. That's correct, isn't it?' Dr. Pollocks said calmly.

The man fired spit. 'Aren't you supposed to wait until I'm dead first?'

'Ah, I see the problem, you didn't read the *whole* of the form *carefully* did you?' the doctor nodded condescendingly, 'The 'death clause', as we doctors call it, of the organ donor agreement doesn't *really* cover thumbs. Their exclusion was a sort of oversight from the 1970s when the document was first drafted, it just never really got done away with – administrators are *busy*, you know – and, well, you had two and the hospital decided that optimum efficiency would be achieved if I had four.'

The man flustered. 'Optimum efficiency?'

'Yes well, it also appears *here*,' he nimbly flipped a page between thumb and thumb, 'that you've been rather unemployed for *quite* some time. The board decided those little devils were going *dreadfully* to waste, my dear chap, and reallocated them to me.'

The man long since knew he was being stolen from. Before his job was sub-contracted to a foreign worker forced to toil longer hours for less money, he would clock into the office each day hours before his boss had arrived, and leave hours after him, yet management would drive away in their *Mercedes* while he had to take the bus. That was how *optimum efficiency* would be reached – incentive, and all that. Well, he couldn't stand for this, stealing his thumbs felt like a bridge too far.

'Look, if you're *awfully* wrapped up in this whole thing,' the doctor added 'then we have a complaints procedure. It's all *very* simple and we could reattach them in two to four weeks, all you need to do is go down to the front desk and they'll take you through it.'

With these last words, the man stared at his hands glumly and nodded. It seemed best not to make more of a scene, if it was in fact possible to civilly resolve the theft.

'Ask for the standard D2-17 form,' Dr. Pollocks said, 'the reception desk is on the ground floor just by the lift, you can't miss it – and best of luck!' He left the room in the wake of a six fingered wave.

After struggling to dress for hours – pulling up his trousers between fingers and palms, zipping his coat between middle and forefinger, and screaming at his shoelaces before ultimately giving up on them – the man walked down to the front desk. The figure sitting behind it reminded him of the early gypsy automatons – the ones you'd slot a coin into to hear your fortune. Her face was covered in a thin veneer of plastic – makeup, he presumed – and her words were reeled out in a digital voice.

'Please take a form from the box: the queue for D2-17s is in corridor five, behind this office,' she said. 'Have a pleasant day and we hope that you are leaving us in good health.'

He nodded at her and ambled his way around the reception to a grey corridor filled with teary men and women, young and old – all scruffily turned out. The process he saw didn't instil much confidence in him. Every three minutes the person at the front of the queue would burst into tears, after which everyone else would inch forward and quietly complain about their predicament.

'This happened to my cousin,' the woman in front of him relayed. 'It was ankles for her though, they call that a D1-18 I think. Got it sorted – right as rain – it will be fine, you'll see.'

He nodded and inched forward, eventually reaching a smiling young administrator.

'Do you have your form?' she beamed.

He handed it to her between his fingers and palm, and she dutifully filled out each section for him, asking questions as she went: name, address, emergency contact details, occupation, salary, marital status, property ownership, and savings account numbers, before handing the form back to him.

'That's perfect, now if you could just sign at the bottom.'

Written in bold letters above the signature box were the words ***please ensure accuracy: signatures will be compared to our database***. He juggled the pen, turning it between his fingers, resting it in different crevices, pulling it into his fist, holding it like a cigarette. Scribbling, erasing, scuffing the page, until he broke down into tears. *Gloves!* He thought, shuddering on the desk as the nurse removed the dampening form from under his head. *God, I'm going to have a hard time buying gloves. I'll buy the regular kind and then cut fingers, I suppose.*

Glass Slider 012 (Blue) by Oliver Canessa

Guinevere

Martha West

I will be honest, it was Pa
Who dragged me on the Eurostar
To gawk at eleven spattered beards
Of vanquished knights, in that Carhaix field.

And the twelfth, with his victorious smirk,
Was to me just another eager jerk
Your highness this, *may I call you Leodegrance* that,
I wished Rience had conquered the prat.

But Daddy was to be won over
And dear Art became my hopeless lover.
His ventures at romance transpired pale,
Let alone the lovemaking. That Holy Flail.

O 'Vere, next to you, bright stars seem dull!
Oh girls, be real, who would have come?
For you, my love, I'd invade the moon
Go ahead, babe. See you soon.

But then
Lackaday!
Lord du Lac!
My pulse: a waning, withering nag
Learnt to canter
Gallop
Heart attack.

First those curls, how they made me glance a lot
That jaw that grin, I was in a trance a lot
His shrewd badinage made me want to chance a lot
His supreme battle feats
Only to enhance the lot

O Lancelot! Lancelot! Lancelot!

Alright, Gwen, baby? Where's your mista?
My pantaloons in hysteria, I, panting, whisper
"Arthur's gone searching for Jesus' platter"
Feverish breath pierces my neck
Chainmail bayonets my shoulders
Searing lips transfix my cheek
Codpiece burns my thighs
I shriek!
"Take me, knight, or I shall shatter!"

Clang
The bassinet hits the floor,

The great helm rolls under the door
I slash the mail coif from his head
As he unsheathes me on the royal bed.

He made me scream on the Round Table,
The kitchen, armoury, anywhere available
Bodice ripping
Tunic ablaze
Farewell to le petite morte d'Arthur days.

Subdue your platitudes of devotion
I can't stand no more dux bellorum boredom
Excalibur can remain frigid in that stone
It takes a Brightkiller
To make this fair queen moan.

What is the Weight of the Moon?

Rohit Chakraborty

Although he was absolutely certain that he would remember every minute of the morning and the afternoon, Doyel nestled on the right side of the Ambassador chomping on a barfi, paranoid that he would forget the dim interiors of the taxi and whatever was being said underneath its blue cushion roof. The colours of the city inundated the car in spurts, like disco lights, then drained, only to have another colour rinse out this vehicle of its ability to remember. First came the ubiquitous orange of the city at dusk in late December, then billboards, of course, then the glittering toys peddled almost everywhere along its veins, then the tube lights from storefronts, and then the explosion of carnival lights in Park Street which made bells swing, reindeer trot, and Santa wave greetings at you. Under the bower of lights which the taxi was gliding under, a procession of horizontal wires which changed colours in waves, the blue shone over the roof, following them until the end of their journey. Their faces were illuminated by the outgoing wave of crimson and the incoming tide of gold.

'What is the weight of the moon?'

'What?' Doyel added with a giggle. He recognised it.

'What is the weight of the moon?' When it was first uttered, Doyel had mistaken the question for an exclamation made in the middle of a fully-formed burp. But Himanta Bordoloi had perfectly imitated the crusty old man in heavy glasses who spelled young graduates' doom before they could defend themselves against such convictions. Not too far, he thought, from everyone who manned every desk at their University. He couldn't wait to be rid of them. 'What is the weight of the moon?'

'You saw it?'

'I did. Now tell me. Wot is thee wait of the moown?'

Himanta was reiterating it purposely. Doyel was sure that he, too, had found the inconsistency of the Bengali accent of the first few words and the affected English "moown" slightly ridiculous. 'Shut up. So did you like it?'

'It was depressing.'

'Why?'

'Because we'll be graduates soon and things are not looking well if what happens in the film is what will happen to us.'

'He's a realist.'

'Who?'

'Ray.'

Their eyes briefly fell upon the rear view mirror, anointed in vermillion, and protected against evil spirits by the swinging column of limes and dry chillies. Neither saw the other on it. Instead, they were both certain that the bloodshot, hooded eyes of the driver were flitting between the road ahead and his passengers.

Crushing the Ganguram box, Himanta leaned against the window, as Doyel was leaning against his, to put to rest any scene which would alarm the driver if it were to play out on his mirror. Doyel was aware of this little arrangement. He imagined himself in one of those prop cars of the black and white decades where the road left behind was a Turner bereft of colour, a staged, bobbing backdrop of the city or the country. The modern world acquainted with new-fangled methods of realism seldom decried how dissociated the stationary interior and the projected world visible through the rear windshield seemed with one another. They had acknowledged its necessity back in the day. We shall suspend our disbelief only briefly. We shall not show on the rear view mirror any evidence other than that of camaraderie and kinship of the most honourable kind which did not manifest itself in the furtive linking of fingers, of Himanta's right and Doyel's left hand, as they turned their gaze away from each other, towards Calcutta.

'What are you thinking about?' Himanta inquired in Assamese.

'The day.' It was terse and in English. Doyel was aware that the city had diluted his father tongue and he was wary about making a fool of himself in front of Himanta, who had taken the Saraighat Express from Guwahati two years ago to escape Cotton College and his Chandmari flat by the foot of the flyover.

'Why?' He asked again in Assamese.

'Memorising it.'

The bequest of Himanta's mother had been the only boon cloaking him and a bane alienating him. Clandestine moments in the dim slices of the evening was when Himanta returned to his language to let passersby, acquaintances, and anybody who stared (and the city is blooming with starers) believe that solemn participation in brotherhood was being had. He was told on his first taxi ride from Howrah to South Calcutta by his mother's brother, who was more than happy to put him up for the entirety of his Bachelor's, that although the languages might have been sisters it did not necessarily rule out the possibility that they could be estranged. He said this, pointing out of the window at every billboard, KTP precautionary hoarding hanging on a streetlamp, and jewellers and confectioners – a Das or a Chatterjee or a Chandra or a Mullick, and Sons. The alphabets were familiar to the eyes but not the ears. 'Non-Bangali?': Mama had acquainted him with the common greeting, only second in its frequency of use to 'What do you want?'. Himanta's monolids, the cream shade of his skin, a Bollywood cadence contending with the Babu Hindi a-la-Pranab Mukherjee, all brought to the fore the inquiry 'Non-Bangali?'. They often said it silently to themselves, intending it as more of an assertion. Within this macrocosm of Bengalis and Non-Bangalis existed a microcosm: prawns and hilsa, Rabi Thakur and Kazi Nazrul, *Bari* and *Basha*. Himanta could occupy the centre and the periphery all at once.

It was always a luxury to ride one of these Ambassadors back home. One of the many ill-kept and firmly clenched heirlooms of the city were these lemon yellow yestercars which now had 'No refusal' painted on their bodies. How could they have taken the rattling steel Metro back home after the golden day they had had? The semester examinations were finally over and it was one more semester and then, in June, they'd be graduates. No refusal. They would now be moving from a semester full of Modernists to a semester full of the Postcolonial. And here they were, at this juncture, walking on the lawns of Victoria Memorial. No refusal. The lawns were peppered with lovers, nibbling faces, tickling skin, in quiet abandon away from the starers of the city. Does the city stifle *your* caresses as well? Doyel had a desire to project a loud question into the warm air hanging around them. No refusal. At nightfall, as they stood close to the gates waiting for an empty taxi because their mobile phones had failed them, the deserted section of the roundabout, the marble lions manning the entry, the sudden gush of chilly breeze, and the awareness of what a rarity days like these were, made them delusional. For a brief moment, the crowd, headlights criss-crossing, the blares of mouths and horns, all dissolved. The residue was that of stationary big cats, freedom fighters on the island in the roundabout, and the monarch behind the gates looking nonplussed as Himanta sidled up to Doyel, and pushed his arm through. They stood with linked arms, one involuntarily rubbing the back of the other's hand with their thumb as if cinema had convinced them that it was the only reflex when it came to acquiring the objects of your affection or intrigue. Then, Himanta leaned in, and muttered, 'Theirs is the morning, noon, and dusk. And ours?' Doyel had wished he could come up with a retort, something along the lines of 'They shut their gates in the evening. We cannot have the night even if we wanted to.' A sudden intrusion, a streak of yellow rushed from their right, slowed, during which Doyel shook Himanta off himself, and halted before them. 'Where do you want to go?' The driver spoke with a Bhojpuri accent. Himanta and Doyel both searched his eyes to see if he had identified them as he drove up to them. Then the noises of the city returned with a crash. A horse-drawn buggy for tourists decked out in Ramanand Sagar finery trod past them. He might as well have asked them 'What is the weight of the moon?'. I might as well have been saying something terribly drab in his ear, Himanta quietly told himself, after all, it's a mela here. The cotton candy man and the bubble through hoops man and a coterie of nuclear familiars suddenly sprung into view. I could have been telling Doyel how horribly maintained the museum was, Himanta told himself, after all, it's a mela here. And so, he leaned towards the window and after fumbling for an answer, which he thought was for a question as ridiculous as the weight of the moon, he said, 'Garia'. Did he see? Does he know? What *is* the weight of the moon? He nodded their admission into the taxi. No refusal.

At the Park Circus Seven Point Crossing, the taxi halted. What had been the faint rumblings of garrulous jockeys on the radio had been suddenly amplified by the driver. Himanta checked the rear view mirror: the driver's eyes did not meet his but looked ahead intensely, with a slight increase in alarm. No sooner had the tapping on Doyel's window pane begun than they ripped their hands away from each other. Her crimson nail against the glass was a gentle gavel against the clamour of the duo on the radio, a male and a female, prefacing one of those grand Bollywood pop singles with tabloid fluff about the actress who was seen lip-synching it in the trailers. Doyel rolled down his window. She was in her Sunday best, a magenta sari and such finery. Her glistening, closely-shaven burnt sienna face produced a weak smile, helpless, to help her case as she put her cupped right hand before Doyel, called him 'Baba', and asked for a tenner in exchange for her benediction. Doyel looked at Himanta whose right hand was now being dragged against his thigh as he had his head turned fully away from the tenor of the pleader. Doyel toyed with the idea of unzipping his backpack and pulling out his wallet. It was not because of the men and women sitting in their Marutis and Toyotas around them watching him, wondering Will he? Won't he? He had felt a sudden dissipation of whatever communion was being had at the back of this taxi when Himanta ripped his hand away. He might as well have decided to ride shotgun for the remainder of the journey: the driver looked on and so did Himanta, as if the lights of the city had no intention of washing out Doyel's recollections but had diluted their hearing instead. He could not tell how Himanta looked but in the rear view mirror such practiced vacancy in the driver's eyes was how the city had taught itself to fend off what were the red light parasites, some of whom sold Pan Parag and crimson cloth for windshields and others who couldn't be bothered. If you pretended not to listen to them, they would go away without you having to say, 'Sorry, I can't help you.' No refusal, indeed. Doyel had the note crunched in his palm when the neon green arrows let engines purr into a rage. She had already left the window, walking away perhaps a little dejected or perhaps with no dejection at all because Doyel had seen so many Calcuttans ignore her and others like her that she must have been used to several hours of empty hands. How could Doyel know about her and her hours? He was riding home in a taxi. What a luxury that was. He put the ten rupee back into his wallet and returned it to his backpack. The car set in motion, the window was rolled up, and Himanta took his hand. Through the half-light he made out Himanta's smile. It had seemed consolatory as if he were telling Doyel, *You mustn't feel like crap. That's how it is*. Doyel did not return the smile. He firmed his grasp on Himanta, took in what was once the White Town through the window, and recited the dying line of a short Stevenson poem quietly to himself: Each a glimpse and gone forever! Each a glimpse and gone forever!

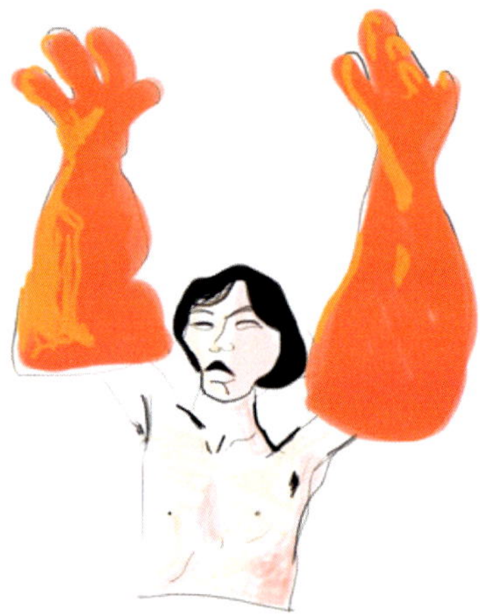

Untitled by Grace Whorrall-Campbell

The Visit

Christy Edwall

At three o'clock, Ginger heard Augustine's knock at the door and felt a zipper of nerves run down her back. She saw with approval the curtains pulled away from the windows, revealing the manicured front lawn she paid Orfeo to tend on one side of the house, and the neighbours' fruit trees on the other. The carpet bore the impress of the vacuum cleaner in long damp stripes, and the house smelled of almonds. The cake had cooled and been iced and now squatted under a glass dome in the middle of her kitchen table as smug as a crystal ball.

When Ginger opened the door, Augustine was standing on the bottom step, her purse tucked firmly under her arm.

I see the hostas are thriving, Augustine said by way of hello.

Oh, hostas, said Ginger. Sometimes I think they're just a weed.

Augustine entered the house. She said nothing about the welcoming aroma of almond. Ginger wondered, in sudden dismay, if Augustine could be allergic to almonds. Nut allergies were on the rise; recipes were changing. At the same time, people were increasingly drinking milk made from nut products. What a world.

How are you? asked Ginger, as she invited Augustine to set down her purse.

Fine, said Augustine, and she kept her purse sandwiched between her thready inner arm and ribcage.

I'll start the coffee, Ginger said, and darted into the kitchen. The chairs were cunningly placed at the dining table to suggest that good friends had been seated in them just a moment before.

Would you like to see the house? asked Ginger when she joined her guest. I've made adjustments. Augustine let herself be led down the hall.

You might notice how little dust there is around the place, Ginger said. I'm a very faithful duster. You might be surprised to know that that was not always the case. I got this dusting mitten you put on your hand. You just stroke the things you want dusted. It just goes right away. If companies advertised their products in this way, they'd make a bucket.

Can you open those cabinets for me, please? said Augustine. Could you move so I could see behind the door?

You'll also notice, I hope, that there is very little clutter, said Ginger. I just read a book on decluttering by a Japanese woman. The Japanese are by nature uncluttered. On the other hand, we are clutter-prone. Maybe our ancestors were not clutter-prone, on account of survival being so perilous. As a result of reading the book, I find that I've been able to get rid of no small number of my possessions that I have no real use for. I give them away to Goodwill. If I was smart, I'd sell them on the internet but arranging the postage is too much for me.

Augustine pulled open the shower curtain to look into the bath. She looked behind the bathroom mirror. She is so thorough, thought Ginger, admiringly. Augustine looked through drawers, through wardrobes, under tables and armchairs. She opened books. She said nothing about the perfectly twinned and rolled paired of socks; nor the clothes arranged by season. Who cleaned Augustine's house? Ginger wondered. It couldn't be Augustine herself. She couldn't shake the vague picture of a man, Augustine's husband, scrubbing the floor on wet knees.

I've rehung a few prints, said Ginger, pointing to pictures she took from a calendar of old travel posters. You might notice a few more candles scattered about. I find that candles at night are more relaxing than a glass of wine.

You haven't been having any wine, have you? said Augustine, sharply, pausing her inspection of Ginger's bedroom.

No, said Ginger, horrified. I wouldn't do that to you.

It's not about me, said Augustine, running her hands under the bed clothes. It's about you. You know that.

I know, said Ginger, humbly.

She was beginning to think that Augustine failed to see the effort she put into the house. She hadn't remarked on the lilacs in the bedroom, or the framed postcard in the bathroom of a man and woman dancing on a beach. Her eyes were cold, like planets; her hands were metal-detectors. Ginger started to remember that perhaps every visit of Augustine's went like this.

The last room Ginger showed her guest was the kitchen. Augustine stood on the threshold of the back door, which overlooked a strip of gravel beneath a pine fence, over which one could see the neighbours' oak trees and the neighbours' parti-coloured garden beds. No children lived at that house. Ginger had tried to liven up the strip of gravel with a few potted plants – cyclamen, calendula, camellia – but she was not a natural gardener. Orfeo refused to have anything to do with potted plants. It was one of his hang-ups.

Do they have grandchildren, your neighbours? Augustine asked.

No, said Ginger, sourly.

I had to ask, said Augustine

The house looks good, she said, after a pause.

Please sit down, said Ginger, gesturing at the amicable chairs. Augustine hesitated for a moment. She seemed to be fighting the urge to check her watch. Good manners prevailed. She sat with a polite smile.

Tea or coffee? Ginger asked.

Coffee.

You take cream, don't you? No sugar?

You have a good memory, said Augustine. Her compliments were like the results of an IQ test.

The coffee was poured; the milk marbled it.

I can tell you're trying hard, said Augustine. You're making progress.

Thank you, said Ginger, Have some cake.

Thank you, said Augustine.

She was not one of those women who looked at a piece of cake on a china plate with poorly disguised greed: those with the beauty of perpetual self-disappointment. There was no want in Augustine's eyes. Her fork sheared off a sliver of the almond cake with iron politeness.

The pause in the conversation consecrated to enthusiastic compliments to the baker passed unfilled. The texture was moist; the almond flakes sprinkled over the icing were perfectly toasted; the rich flavours of the cake crested in Ginger's mouth. And still Augustine went on eating as the dead eat, making a show for the living.

Augustine set down her fork on the side of her neglected cake. It must be lonely here, she said, probing.

Ginger didn't answer.

Have you been out of the house for recreational purposes? Augustine asked. Perhaps you went to a party, or to the beach? You know not all of those places are safe for you.

When Augustine was absent, Ginger imagined her visits. These visits were hearty, confessional. Augustine's immaculate grooming became disheveled and her advice was unwise but greathearted. Whereas the real Augustine, the one sitting at the kitchen table, was the kind of woman that kept her kitchen spices in identical, hand-labeled glass vials. She knew how dry-cleaning worked and never spent money on pumpkin lattes in October. Why did Ginger want Augustine to like her? It would be like having an eagle as a friend. You'd always be looking at its talons.

I don't really go outside, Ginger said, humbly. I've been experimenting with online grocery shopping and food delivery.

Oh? said Augustine, scalping off another shaving of cake.

Yes, said Ginger. The strange thing is, I always get the same delivery man. Whether I order the delivery on a weekday or a weekend, the early morning or late at night, it's the same man. I almost say, Oh you again? I almost ask his name. If you see someone once a week, you probably ought to know their name. On the other hand, I think he's heard something about me. He stares. In fact, he reminds me of a shark. Not a big shark like a great white shark, but a smaller shark, with a smaller mouth and bigger teeth.

It sounds a little paranoid, Augustine said, after a pause.

Maybe I'll try another service: one that costs a little more but teaches its employees not to stare at customers.

You can't keep people from knowing, Augustine said. Your case was very public. It was in all the newspapers.

It's been nearly two years, said Ginger. Surely someone else has made a mistake by now.

Augustine chewed carefully. Ginger knew she didn't like discussing Ginger's history in terms of mistakes. Mistakes were made in chemistry tests, not in what Augustine called *life choices*. You had to take responsibility for your actions. But that is exactly what it was, a mistake: when it had come to the affair with Chris, Ginger had not had all the information. That is, she had purposefully forgotten half of what she ought to have known, like his age, and underestimated the seriousness of the rest, like the law. It was like overestimating how far your car could go on an empty fuel tank. You didn't really know the capacity of the engine until you were stranded.

More coffee? Ginger asked.

No, thank you, said her guest.

Ginger, reckless, poured herself another cup like it was whiskey, and she cut herself another slice of cake.

Augustine hadn't said anything about how much trouble Ginger had taken with her appearance or the new dress: white, with sprigs of cherry blossom taken from the print of a nineteenth-century French gardener's manual.

Have you heard from your children? asked Augustine. Have they come to see you?

No, said Ginger, of course not. No.

Can I see a picture? said Augustine.

Ginger walked slowly to her bedroom and took an old picture from the side table, a staged family photograph taken for a Christmas card, of Lily and Adam when they had the natural corruption of six-year-olds and could be arranged in photos with bribes.

Is this the only one? said Augustine, returning the photograph.

I don't think I need to remind you how important it is for you to keep doing what you're doing, said Augustine, when Ginger returned from replacing her single icon, deflated. You're doing very well. Better, I'd say, than my other cases. No one's more surprised than I. When you came here you were a mess. My visits were, to say the least, exhausting. But you have come far. You are rebuilding your life. You're lucky.

Lucky, repeated Ginger flatly.

A silence fell.

I must go, the guest said, and stood up. I have other cases to see.

Ginger stood mechanically to accompany Augustine to the door.

One more thing, said Augustine, in the living room. Before I forget.

She bent over Ginger's foot and took the heavy black anklet in her hands.

It looks fine, she said. When it's time for a battery replacement, the Department will be notified and they'll send someone over.

The previous week, Ginger had gone to the movies for a matinee in stilettos, a red ribbon wrapped around the anklet like a May Day garland to match the anklet's small blinking light. She picked a film that had been out for two weeks and had the theatre to herself. The cleaners she passed on her way in and out of the theater stared at her anklet. They said nothing to her but spoke to each other in their own language.

Augustine stood up. I'll see you next month, she said, closing the door behind as though it were a cell door. Ginger stood in the still house. She heard the sound of Augustine's engine turning, catching, and then fading away. It seemed that all the cars in the neighbourhood had driven away. Nothing in the air but the spaces in between bird calls.

Ginger walked to the kitchen, picked up her almond cake, and tweezing open the garbage with her foot on the lever at the base, threw it into the mouth of the can. She sat at the table. The birds in the neighbours' garden sang from their free perch in the oak. She stood again. Her neighbour was in the garden. He had brought out a portable radio and switched it on: traffic accidents, a gas leak, a recall of votes, and to follow, a lovely late quartet.

She walked to the garbage can, stood on the lever, and stared down at the ruined cake. It had fallen so that the icing was still visible; the almonds were just beginning to slide down the sagging sides. Then she reached down, scooped a still-warm handful of almond cakeflesh, and began, in triumph, to eat.

Mother becomes Infatuated with Typewriter Ribbon

Lucy Tiller

Mother, at the village jumble sale, buys 12 spools
of typewriter ribbon. "I just love the colours",
she says, and decorates picture frames
with black and red in the beige hallway.

Six days later, she unpacks a cardboard box
on the kitchen table. "It's okay," she says.
"They're only £2.75 per spool on eBay."
The morning melts in her hands.

The drawer in the garage, marked mother, blooms
into a whole garage. "Nobody cycles anyway,"
she says, as she throws the bikes onto next door's skip,
a hint of black-and-red slipping from her jeans pocket.

Returning from work once, I find her lying
on the bedroom floor, ribbons hanging down
from her ears like seaweed from mermaids,
tucked neatly among swathes of spools, and

she asks if she can borrow some money.
When I tell her I'm not funding her habit she
throws a neat cylinder at me, and as it sha-
tters on my hip, my mother begins to unravel into tears.

Mother has not eaten in 46 hours, pastes herself
with typewriter ribbon and giggles as it tickles her
naked skin, wraps it around her head as bandages
to stop her day job bleeding.

Later, we leave home for university. My sister
wonders if we should call in professional help.
One day, in her own home, Mother is found
beneath the rubble of some collapsed factory,

barely breathing.

Finland

Antonia Cundy

So many things about Finland were blue. The berries, the hire car, the sea, the thick card of my book's cover, the sky. I even used a blue pen to tattoo their memories onto the pages of my notebook (the notebook, though, was orange). Writing after breakfast, I realised that the blueberries I had sprinkled on our yoghurt bowls that morning had stained my fingers. They'd left reddish-blue blots over my fingertips; small blooms of mottled, mulberry burns. At home, blueberries are fat, waxen balls that widen around the middle. But the blueberries in Finland were small, their skin as thin and sheer as cranberries'. They were shiny and slippery, perfectly circular little beads full of a sharp, purple blood. My wet fingertips pressed fingerprints into the page, and it wasn't clear what was ink and what was blueberry juice.

It was an August morning in Helsinki, and the sun was piercing. It threw health into the streets like a deluge of rain, clearing the cityscape so used to the dark and flooding it instead with a brilliant, blue light. It professed a faith in summer's redemption as strong as that which some see in the Virgin blue of Mary, who watches over the city in the jade steeples of Uspenski, the Orthodox cathedral dedicated to her assumption. Yet I knew, from the Lakeland, that this Finnish blue was a shapeshifter – it might, at night, turn black and bottomless. I'd watched it do just that when we swam, naked, in a lake near Savonlinna. The lake was only ours for twenty-four hours, but not a single other person ever shared our big blue bath, not as a nearby bather nor as a dot on the horizon. If it weren't for seventeen other happy reviews on Airbnb, the romantic inside me might imagine the lake only ever appeared for us, and that the forest drank it back up when our little Skoda drove away.

In a rowing boat out on the lake, it was the water that let us know that night was coming, not the sky. As the sun slowly fell and the sky slipped on a dusky grey dress, the lake acted twice as fast. It drew thick, black shutters underneath its surface, closing off the sparkling transparent blue that had all day left an open view down to the lake's deep bed, its seagrass carpet. The moon appeared, reflected, where previously the sun's rays had filtered through. My toes, dangling over the boat's edge, no longer distorted underwater into rippled versions of themselves, but disappeared and reappeared, volunteers in a vanishing act each time a dark swell lapped at them. When we reached the shore, we pulled our rowing boat up onto the sand, and leaving our clothes by the fire we walked back out into the dark water. Someone once told me that if you magnify black ink enough, zoom in far closer than the human eye can do alone, the pigment actually turns out to be blue. I don't know if it's true, but when I stared at the lake's black liquid, it too, slowly turned blue. We waded out until the water's chilly hug reached our waists, then sank down, swimming into the deep blue dark. Up close, the night-water wasn't as opaque as it had seemed from the boat. My arms glowed through the surface in front of me, tinged slightly yellow-green by the darkness. We swam until the water felt warm and the fire that we'd left kindling on the shore had fanned itself up into flames, its fiery hands waving at us to come back, to sit by its side. My milky, citrus limbs trod water beneath me as I looked out into the centre of the lake. In Finnish, the word 'peninkulma' is used to describe a Scandinavian mile, a distance of ten kilometres. But this definition is a modern standardisation – its meaning used to be based on its archaic etymology, 'peni' for 'dog', and 'kuuluma', which roughly translates into English as 'to be heard'. Years ago, it meant the distance over which a dog's bark could be heard in still air. Looking out over the lake, where I could no longer distinguish between the sky and the water, or see its forested edge, I wondered how many *peninkulmas* lay between us and the other side.

Back onshore, we filled a bucket from the lake's shallows and ladled the water onto the sauna's hot coals. As it hit them, it hissed upwards into a hot mist. Lying down on the warm pine, the cold lake-drops left on our naked bodies evaporated in the heat of their lake's own, coal-made steam. As summer returns to winter, in Finnish summer cabins, the sauna's steaming little heart is what keeps away the cobwebs, turning freezing water into a warming, airborne bath. Built away from the cabin itself, on decking right down by the water's edge, our sauna was like a wooden waiting room, a liminal world where wet air accustomed our bodies to the transition between water and sky, the lake and the land. Through the glass doorway, the lake looked black, not blue, once more. Beads of sweat started to drop into the freshwater puddle left by my wet hair, and the remnants of the lake's inky hues slowly faded from my feet, as pinks and reds warmed themselves back into the mottled blue skin.

In the bright sunlight of Helsinki, I wondered what it would be like to be at the cabin in June, when the nights in Finland are white, not black. Would the lake turn white at night too? I'd thought August's sixteen-hour sunlight, its eleven o'clock sunsets, were bright with life enough for anyone, but for Finns who know June, August is autumnal. Tove Jansson writes about the month in *The Summer Book*, her novel set on an island in the Gulf of Finland, where she used to go as a child every Finnish summer:

> Every year, the bright Scandinavian summer nights fade without anyone's noticing [...] It is still summer, but the summer is no longer alive. It has come to a standstill; nothing withers, and fall is not ready to begin. There are no stars yet, just darkness.

I thought back to our sauna, that liminal mist that we'd lain in, unaware. Unaware that the season was liminal too, that we had caught our cabin in the darkness between white nights and the stars.

On the Helsinki balcony that morning, thinking about the lake's black and blue world, I'd written a poem from thoughts that rippled through my mind in patterns that prose would not follow. One night on a limitless lake and one poem – ashamed, I thought of how Jansson had written an entire book, set a story over a long, white summer, on an island so small it took only four and a half minutes to walk around its edge. Jansson's limitless vision of her island reminded me of a conversation I had had with Pertti, a sixty-eight-year-old Finn whose house we stayed in on the Nauvo archipelago. He spoke about why he had decided to leave Helsinki, and move to the islands where the land is slowly lost to the sea. 'The islands are exhaustive, see,' he said. 'The forests, the sea, my garden, boating, foraging... it's endless. Helsinki... Well, Helsinki exhausted me.' That evening, Pertti cooked a fresh salmon for us, a huge fish with flesh so orange it could have been alive. He served it with bitter herbs he had picked in the woods, where blueberries grow like weeds. I had never known salmon could taste so strong. Pertti chuckled over our astounded reactions. 'Yes!' he said, 'yes, that is what salmon tastes like!' He laughed with his whole body, dropping a chunk of the glowing flesh he was helping himself to more of. Pertti talked late into the night with us and the other guests, his hands resting on a belly full of salmon and wine, and blueberries which had gone to his eyes, where they glistened wet and dark with laughter. Later, in bed, in lines of blue ink, I wrote the salmon's orange flesh into the pages underneath my notebook's orange cover. When we woke in the morning, we ate breakfast on the wooden terrace and the sun sparkled so brightly off the sea it filtered my whole view through a diamond of white.

My vision fractured into diamonds too on the balcony in Helsinki, as the sunlight caught the face of my watch and glanced up into my eyes. I took a break from the poem to look out at the block of flats opposite, whose white and grey squares met the blue sky as sharply as if they had been cut onto a green screen set to blue. It hadn't been enough for Pertti, but even in Helsinki I had found traces of his islands' exhaustive nature. Looping one afternoon around the city park, we found a café that sat on the rocks high above a lake, where paddle boarders wobbled the water's body below. Its wooden boarding was painted the same light blue as Pertti's house and our Lakeland cabin. On the top floor, a white balcony cupped the full-length windows, supporting the awning with regular white poles. The intersecting white and blue lines divided the top floor up like a series of wooden Finnish flags, unintentional expressions of pride watching over their waterfront. Down beneath the terrace, the rocks held onto the last of the sun's lingering fingers. Long tufts of elephant grass sprung up like furry ears between their grey, bouldering heads, liver-spotted with moss and lichen. Sitting there, with the café behind us, and another vast expanse of sparkling blue in front, we could have been about to slip into the sauna, or sit down to a salmon dinner.

My now empty yoghurt bowl had interested two hungry ants, who sucked at the milky blue swathes left around the edge. Their antennae danced disjointedly above them, out of time with the music I played through my speakers – the soft song of Audrey Hepburn singing 'Moon River'. My poem was an inky mess; scratchings out and scribbles that fell from page to page. I wrote it out neatly on a new, clean sheet.

Ayuthaya

Florence Ward

Sometimes when she had writer's block she'd change her font, pick a new one that she hadn't used before. Times New Roman had become overdone. It was frigid and didn't let her say exactly what she wanted. And anyway, when she wrote by hand she never drew her 'a's like that, so it was dishonest. Currently, she liked one called 'Ayuthaya' that made her think of typewriters, and made her words seem much more precious because of it. She did buy a type-writer once, but it frustrated her, and she went through pots of Tipp-Ex at an economically unwise rate.

Today she sat in front of her laptop and wrote the first line in Ayuthaya, and then stopped and made a cup of coffee. Rasheed was going to work, but he was making a meal of it, and she had been hearing the sound of him – packing his bag, going upstairs to fetch something he'd forgotten four or five times, putting on his coat, his hat, checking he had his keys – for the past fifteen minutes. She couldn't concentrate with the noise. She did an internet search and discovered that Ayuthaya was designed in 1992, and was named after the capital of the Siamese kingdom that existed between 1351 and 1767.

'I'm leaving.'

Its main purpose was clarity, and it would be difficult to confuse a capital 'O' with a zero.

'Babe, I'm going to work,' Rasheed called, ever patient, always erasing what he'd said before instead of building on it. She didn't look up but she told him to have a good day. Rasheed left and closed the door quietly behind him. She thought, briefly, about how Rasheed's days were never exceptionally good, and if they were good it was never because of his job, which was to be in charge of the forklift at a Sainsbury's depot about an hour's bus ride away from home. She knew he liked Matt, who he worked with most of the time, and didn't like his boss, who was passive aggressive. Rasheed wasn't so much open as he was unlocked; what you couldn't see from the outside of him was easy enough to access. Her father called him *a simple man* and she could tell that, with Dad, this was a good thing.

After finishing her cup of coffee, she put the kettle on again, and sat down in front of her laptop. She wrote two more lines. The other week, she'd watched a documentary about sharks and learnt a lot about their biology. *Like sharks, your skin is made of teeth, and I am bleeding for days after we have sex.* She thought this was inspired. With practised hands she put the coffee granules in the cafetiere and poured the water in, put the press on top so that it sat perfectly above the water line. She sat down again, decided that *have sex* was too tame and should be changed to *fuck*, and then checked her phone.

At five to ten, her mother called.

'Your cousin has gone into labour. This morning, at about six, apparently. I think it's all going well.'

'That's good, Mum,' she said, wondering whether *fuck* was perhaps too obvious. Maybe it shouldn't be sex at all. It is, she supposed, perfectly plausible to bleed from sex and that fact defeated the point of the metaphor. No, instead she would change it, when the phone call finished, to *I am bleeding for days after we touch.*

'Are you ok?'

'Yes, Mum,' she said.

'Oh, well, there's a lot of things to look forward to,' her mother continued, as if she hadn't believed her. 'Hannah's birthday on the fifth – you are coming to the restaurant aren't you? – and then of course it's going to be exciting when Dad starts working on this new film. And the baby. I really think you should send a little gift – I know you're a bit skint at the moment, but just something little would be nice, a little toy or something.'

'I'm not skint,' she said.

'Oh, well, these things don't have to be expensive. A little toy or something, and a card, it's the thought that counts isn't it?'

'I've got to go, Mum,' she said, 'it's been nice talking. I'll see you soon.'

'At the restaurant for Hannah's?'

'Yes. Bye.'

At her laptop, she changed *fuck* to *touch*, and wondered what Rasheed was up to. He would be excited about the baby, and about being an uncle, even though he already had six or seven nieces and nephews. Rasheed had a lot of siblings, and she had the private suspicion that they all disliked her, found her boring and unskilled at conversation. She found them brash, but good dancers.

From the John Lewis website, she bought a soft toy rabbit, grey with pink on the insides of its ears, and paid £20.85 including postage. She hoped the price would show up in the quality of the fur.

Like sharks,
your skin is made of teeth,
and I am bleeding for days after we touch.
The blood is in my cuticles
and no matter how many times I wash my hands;
I have become the Scottish king's wife.

Harry, who she had met at a writers group, told her that referencing Shakespeare was always a winning hand. She thought this odd, and slightly counter-intuitive advice, but remembered all of what she'd learnt when studying *Macbeth* in year twelve, and thought that last line in particular sounded allusive and impressive. Reminded of Harry, she looked at his Facebook on her phone, and then looked at the Facebook of his girlfriend, and was pleased to find her objectively less attractive than herself.

At one-thirty, Rasheed texted. He was on his lunch break and wanted to know how her day was going. *Hey babe, how are you getting on? I hope you've written loads of poems by now!* She thought his ignorance – about the process of writing, how torturous it was, how long it took for the words to even make it on to the page (or the screen) – endearing instead of irritating. Her mother often commented that Rasheed (and, more pointedly, Rasheed's *family*) would like it if she got a job, just temporarily of course, until she got recognised as a poet, but this was only because she didn't understand that Rasheed didn't mind. She texted back that it was going well, and that the poem was probably nearly finished, and was maybe her best work yet.

I wear gloves to lunch,
But my sister knows we've fucked,
And tells me I make bad decisions.

She thought about Hannah's birthday lunch on Thursday and how unlike her poem it would be. Far from the fact that her entire extended family loved Rasheed, – they thought him, she suspected, dangerously exotic – Hannah and her had never got on well enough to the point of using the word *fucked.* When she was seventeen, she'd gone into her big sister's room and told her she'd *had sex* with Billy, and Hannah had said well done and asked if she needed condoms. It was one of the most intimate moments they'd shared.

In fact, the poem wasn't really about Rasheed at all. Rasheed's hands had never made her bleed, not even literally. Rasheed's hands were strong and could put up shelves, open jars, bench 300lbs. But they didn't make her bleed in the sense that the man in the poem's had, her whole body throbbing. She hadn't slept for days after they'd touched, had sat awake shivering in the December cold and watching Netflix into the small hours, checking her phone at every scene change. She had thought that all the male characters looked like him, each one more than the one before, and eventually this constant reminding exhausted her so much she passed out on the sofa, and woke up wearing the same clothes and with a food stain on her chin.

No, Rasheed wasn't like that, but she knew his gentleness and the way he insisted on changing sheets after every time must be good qualities.

It was four o'clock. She got an email from John Lewis saying her payment had been declined. She tried to write another line but couldn't think of anything to come after the *bad decisions* and thought that maybe it had a finality to it that didn't need any more. She closed her laptop.

When Rasheed came home and read the poem he asked her why it was so violent.

'It's love,' she said, and then, 'and it's a metaphor. Not real violence, just the way love feels sometimes, you know?'

'Did I ever make you feel this way, make you bleed?' He was concerned.

'It's not autobiographical,' she said.

They ate soup for dinner, which she heated up, and her mother called to say the baby had been born, and was a boy, and was probably going to be called Harry. She thought about Harry from the writers group and whether his hands could make her bleed.

'Are you going to get the poem published?'

She had bread in her mouth and waited until she had finished chewing to answer.

'You can't just *get* something published. But I will try.'

'I see.'

She ate some more of her soup. 'Do you like it? The poem, I mean.'

'I think it's very violent, but then, what do I know about these things?' said Rasheed, and he took his bowl and bread plate to the sink and washed them up. She watched his soapy hands perform this action. That evening, whilst he had a bath, she changed the font of her poem to 'Windings 2' and stared at the screen until the lines of symbols bore themselves into her head.

Build by Joy Hunter

Oldest Song

Minying Huang

after sà fú[1]

ancient zither, slender.
sleeping girl, gentle footfall
in my ear. reed between
lips sits casual, pensive. your
chest falls
like sun on snow.

vibrato, rich honey,
rises over villages spun
from silk, which swathe your
arms,
sure touch.

early morning.
villagers of a lady's robe
stir, spilling
myth into this gaze I carry
with me when

I think of you. breeze
of chord strike, fragrant sage,
jolts delicate, extracts
whistle of the
player.

cháng'é[2] chose the moon,
fruit, and cake,
blesses bearers of pastry
with beauty

1 Phonetic Chinese for Sappho
2 Chinese goddess of the moon

so that they may
share in elixir (as you are
to me),

so that she may listen,
strung up in satellite,

to love.

Crane Bag

Katherine Robinson

Thou shalt be two hundred white years… a crane. A good vessel of treasures will be made of thy skin.

Lays of Fionn, curse laid on the sea god's wife.
(John Mac Neill, translator)

I.

He lifted the body, death-swollen,
taut, its tidy feathers
encasing the cold

uncoiling from inside her.
Her long neck extended straight out
like a dowser pointing to water

and water and more water,
the spreading sea he'd rule forever.
He slashed her open, undid tackles of crimped guts;

her ribs bowed
out, a busted trap
shagged with rust and blood –

that animal had dragged
itself free long ago. He peeled her skin back
like a jacket and sewed it into a bag.

Still nothing was quiet:
her wings beating
in the waves' thud and keening, desperate,

faint, just past the shrieks of gulls.
Exhausted, he slept with feathers heaped around him
and hands webbed with blood.

II.

He cinched the bag closed around his hoard
of treasures: bolts of the moth-spun wind,
a whale-skin belt embroidered

with seaweed, a gold boat with oars hammered sheer
as maple seeds,
a lantern made from the burnished skull of a seal.

He lay on the sand in the scent of brine,
holding the bag and felt it
empty in his hands until it was a pile of flat hide:

all he'd stowed was gone
by sunset, then, inexplicably, back
when the morning tide slouched in.

III.

Grief turned all he loved intermittent.
He could hear, far away, her discarded wings
unsorting the dark as the cured,

hollow body in his arms filled and emptied
again and again, immune
to the fancy knotwork he tied,

and the crane was calling him to follow,
her raw voice in the waves's cough,
hoarse and still calling

to where he stood by the ocean
he ruled, a god
who contained what he loved by feeling it vanish.

He'd watched the bird two centuries,
wanting the woman she'd been.
Just past what he could conquer,

loss changed shapes. He held the empty skin of a bird
against his chest all night,
waiting for whatever could return.

A Boy with Autism/Eggshell

William Skelton

like a bird/but also like a shell
You are hunched and fragile, close-winged
tight gripping claws of little scales on dead branches.
but You are not a bird
You make Yourself a nest/amongst the speaker wires
all tangled like neurones/like thoughts pressing
on the inside of Your head.
not yet hatched, no feathers means no flight
nor whistling in air.

You sit in Your room in Your room in Your room You sit/where The Darkness is
in Your room/where The Light isn't
Where Your computer glow serves Your photosynthesis.

In Your songs Your songs the songs You're in/
the language instinct does not possess You
it is not Your possession-
flames have tongues and so do You-
rather/all the words
You made are pre-programmed and synthesised:
a composition of a conversation:
Syntax and hymnal/for melody.

tiny like an electron an electron/like an electron You are tiny
You have been understood
by Your invisibility and indivisibility and we measure You with microscopes
the smallest of steps is progress.
progress is the smallest of steps.

but You are not an electron. You are like dark matter, unseen, absent,
but there. You are there, absolutely there, detected by the faintest of signals,
floorboards whispering/doors closing.
but You are not dark matter You are no more faith than You are physics
but We believe. We believe.
We have to. We believe.

The Gathering by Luke Dawes

The Prevention Of

Mary Anne Clark

The train is looking away when the station
stops moving and then it's gone. The eye of
the needle is looking away. The eye of the
storm is looking away. I've got eyes in the
back of my head, said the pillow to a
smaller pillow, looking away. The wind
is looking away, brushing against a whole
street of houses with their eyes shut and
not even noticing. The drunk man vomiting
is looking away and the drunk man
not vomiting is looking away. The stars
are looking away, not because they're
crying. The door and the door handle
are looking away. The sky is looking
away, looking very away and very thin.
I've got my eye on you, said the moon, but
it hadn't.

Montezuma: King of Blackburn

James Golding

There is nothing but the word, the mulch.
I leave my weapons outside the door,
I need only sharp thoughts, honed by you
for skinning cats. Only my nose betrays me.

The banners bedeck King George's Hall,
and Barbara Castle Way is thick with flowers.
When the new king enters in triumph along
the A666, the people do not disappoint us.

Now indeed the word is made flesh. He is
every inch the northern Christ, the pole star.
His rising brings them all, their frenzy, speaking
tongues outside fire-gutted betting shops.

And we, the lieutenants: are we not also
touched by divinity? In this new dawn, shall we
not also take our share? From every man his tongue,
his hands: to speak our voice, to do our work.

Stack the bodies high in Eanam Wharf; to make
an omelette you must break some skulls. The
barges chug them from our kingdom with stolid
constancy, crewed by true, stout-hearted men.

The mob demands flesh. Thus, from Beardwood
to Whinny Heights let the proclamation sound:
There shall be feasting in the streets, let every kebab
shop door be thrown wide in the blazing argon light.

Only the angels now can save us from ourselves.
Smoke rises from bone cold mill chimneys, gaping.
Our bywords shall be clod, and death, and mettle;
our eyes will seek the swiftly rising sun.

Hail Montezuma, King of Blackburn. May our
desperate throats turn hoarse. May gentle tears fall
on our crops. May the moon shatter and drift down
like paper, like poems, like doner from heaven.

Sophie, Oxfordshire, 1620 by Elaine Robertson

Curve

Susan Maginn

Breast feel swollen, heavy, like pregnant pause,
Like autumn falling, like solemn lie.
Breast larger pray mama don't notice,
We all know what this means she say.
Orange to grapefruit, hands cupping, pressing
For lumps, no dimple, no smudge.
It is fresh juice, it is light touch, it is too much
Fruit imagery here let's try something new.

Do you see the way birds fly? And the spine
Of 阿公 eighty years old? And the snail home
Perched on saliva? And can you connect the dots?
The newspaper lady in another short story
Mine; the dog tail yawning; the post flying
Across the lawn. It is the shape of back arching
Mouth gasping pink hot lips pucker.
It is the colour of sweat trickling sun
Beam sand tickling small feet.

The Merchant's Wife

Harriet David

She put her tongue upon my
breast. Her gums were
awful red. I took my dresses
in. She was heroic, like
a ceiling, done in cream
with pink illuminating
elbows, dimpled knees.

All summer long I smelled
of sour cheese. How beautiful
you daughter is, they said.
I agreed. Your father sends
you silk, I said, wrapped
in patchouli leaves. A rattle
carved in fretwork ivory.

A wet-nurse was unfashionable.
She gnawed at me. See, I said,
ambergris. Jars of sweet ginger.
Silver beads. Rich things a
shipwreck might have left
under the big grey sea. She
put her tongue upon my breast.

Her gums were awful, red.
I'll pack you up, sweet,
crystallised. You'll smell of flat
pink knees. Of ivory. A sea
is closing over me,
I said. She put her tongue
upon my breast. *Agreed.*

For Later

Harriet David

I know you keep some years
inside your cheek, safe,
wadded up against your teeth

I did the same with white bread
as a child. Wait long enough,
the enzymes turn it sweet

you'll tell me if that happens,
I suppose. Is it your girlhood
that you chose to keep

the years you spent abroad
that other man? The day you swam
through chilly flanks of kelp, so deep

I thought I'd never see you break
the dazzle? The things you took
and didn't tell, the heap

of broken walnut shells
the water glass, the summer smell
the plate of oily meat?

I know it's not the orange
tablecloth, the wine, us touching and
untouching, underneath.

I know you, raw as any novice
thief. You flinch away
you chew, you watch your feet

one day I'll turn to you
my love, open your mouth
and eat.

Untitled 3 by Sophia Spralja

Hangover

Lucy Tiller

heavy with the smell of last night's red wine he comes
to drink my earl grey tea, drop into the soft treading of dreams –
with me, some cotton-wool comfort blanket, among his arms –

gather pity with a lint roller from the outsides of my jeans,
mutter the soft underbellies of nothing through the shallow waters
of morning sleep, still hidden within his college scarf, still

wrapped in air and arms and the mists of nearby pubs, and i
watch the slow drift of his eyelids, like dust in august.
pathetic, limp as a damp splitting teabag, he tells me

that he must leave as he buries himself deeper into my pillow,
draped over the prongs of a headache, the mug of tea cooling
and hardening into a milk-skinned soup.

and it is my desire to laugh at him, but his eyelashes tremble
like dream-catchers, and trap each breath like moths,
painting flickering shadow puppets upon the walls, shivering with the light –

Bath

Katherine Robinson

All night I swabbed a sponge across your lips.
Your dry mouth closed and relaxed.
Water was the last thing your body knew to want.

For days, you fought the fluid building in your throat,
your breath a jagged rasp that filled the room.
Your doctor called it 'death rattle':
strange instrument that shook your body
until it merged with you and quieted.

I wash your shoulders and neck,
wash the furrows around your eyes and close them.
You look just as you always have.
I pour birch oil into my palm
and rub it onto your cooling forehead.
The dead are anointed out of fear
the spirit won't realize any change
has happened and will, bewildered, anxious,
wait beside a body less and less its own.

I keep talking as I pour oil into my hands
until they are the sheen of the sea you loved,
endlessly cresting off the gray Maine coast,
and I place my hands on your forehead,
and it's the sheen of white weathered birch trees,
and I'm still talking as I pour the oil
although it's no longer you I'm talking to.

Number Eight

Alannah Lewis

Number Six is a modest mansion. Double-fronted. Ambassador's white. Boot-scrapers ensconced by the front door. You must pass Number Six if you want to get to Number Eight. It is the law of basic mathematics and of English house numbering. Number Eight was Ms Driscoll's. It had been a caretaker's cottage before she bought it. She had not known the caretaker.

My mother (she wasn't my mother then) found Number Eight easily. It was by far the smallest house on Abbotsbury Road. Stridently stone-clad with dirty window boxes. Two-storied. There was a kitchen and small bedroom and an airy room that would have once been called a 'parlour'. Any of them would have done, but Ms Driscoll told her to take the photo in the attic because the light was good. It was winter then. The day began at nine in the morning, and dribbled out by noon. They would have to be quick. Not least of all because Ms Driscoll was going to die.

***

A long time before she had me, my mother worked for a small and optimistic company which shot portraits of the terminally ill. They called them "still lifers" in the industry, the industry being roughly not-many people in a workshop in Ealing, and a rudimentary web-page in the days of dial-up internet. They did other kinds; pregnancy portraits, graduation portraits, portraits of pedigree Shih-Tzus. Photographing the terminally ill was most lucrative though, because the terminally ill were in high demand. Policy stipulated that portraits would be sat for and taken in just the one sitting (Twenty Four Hour Turn-Around Or Your Money Back!) and the portrait, once dipped in salt-and-vinegar developing chemical and hung out to dry on a washing line as delicately as a pair of knickers, would be posted to a well-paying family member or friend for whom, if it was too late to see their loved one at their best, would gladly take them at their last. Portraits of the terminally ill, my mother found out, were never for the terminally ill.

Ms Driscoll didn't have any children. She said that she never liked the idea of making and growing something for the specific purpose of it outliving you. Girls in her day were squeezing them out in a post-war panic, the young left to rear the young. Ms Driscoll could never bear to be predictable. She did not like people who were too easy to read. Nor did she like translucent shower-curtains, nor violins. She *did* like five o'clock Sidecars and handsome men such as Paul Newman. She told my mother all this within five minutes of her arriving at Number Eight, twenty years ago. Ms Driscoll's palliative radiotherapy course sometimes left her uninhibited. Overcast and insensible, she'd have days when she'd bump against the corners of her own home, eating everything that she found in sight from pickled eggs to soup powder. She had called her nephew one morning with some complaint about a ghost in the house, only to realise that the fat white creature she had seen passing by the reflective microwave door was in fact herself.

My mother lived ten minutes away from Abbotsbury Road, in a flat opposite Shepherd's Bush train station. The walk to Mrs Driscoll's house that morning would be short, but sufficiently painful; her trainers, stuck with frost, became tighter and tighter as her cold feet swelled and sweated within them. Whilst the Montessori school-children in their dove-grey and bottle greens raced towards their Victorian school houses, and the frozen rough-sleepers slept, my mother replayed the conversation she had had with Ms Driscoll over the phone a week earlier.

***

'Tasteful, mind. Nothing gaudy. They're for private... *perusal*. I hear your company specialise in photographing the sick in their last days? Well, I don't know about *last* days. But it's never a bad thing to take stock of your tomorrows, is it?'

'No, I... I suppose not. And you're absolutely sure that's what you want?'

'Unconditionally.'

'Can I take a name?'

A crackle.

'You do understand what I'm getting at, don't you?'

'Absolutely I do... Ms--?'

'Driscoll. You are capable? Experienced?'

'Oh yes. Very.'

'Now, what do you say about the twenty-sixth? Nine o'clock? Get a pen and I'll give you my address.'

***

During her walk, my mother had drawn up a face from that voice. Long, horsey, intellectual. A real Bloomsbury face. This was not the face which answered the door.

'Ms Driscoll? I'm Christina? From Plaistow Portraits? You have an appointment with us for nine o'clock?'

'Tomorrow.'

'Beg your pardon?'

'I'm expecting you tomorrow. Thursday.'

'I have here Wednesday?'

'Oh. Well now's good as any time.'

What had seemed to be a clipped broadcaster's accent over the phone on second-thoughts possessed that nasal quality common to alumnae of the Northern grammar-schools. There were traces of ironed-out dialect. She pronounced her 'Thursdays' as 'Thursdees'. She was small, my mother thought, probably even smaller without any hair on her head. Ms Driscoll could not have been much older than fifty either, although it was hard to say exactly, my mother being cursed with that young person's inability to gauge the age of anyone older than herself.

'You were the girl I spoke to on the phone?'

'Yes. That was me.'

'Then you know the sort of thing I'm after? You've done this sort of thing before?'

'Yes. In some capacity.'

'Is that meant to fill me with confidence?'

'Sorry. I mean, yes. Yes, I know what I'm doing.'

'Better that time.'

***

Ms Driscoll was the one who suggested the attic. When they got there, she began to take off her clothes. There were not many to take off. She had been gowned in only a seersucker housecoat when she answered the door. My mother, averting her eyes, pretended that the lens was playing up for a while.

'I don't mind you watching, you know. Girls your age never get to see bodies like mine.'

'Oh! That's… that's fine!' said my mother. 'I'm just sorting out the, er, the aperture.'

'Sounds very technical.'

'Oh yes, *very*!' my mother said downwardly, reassuring no-one but her shoelaces.

'How would you like me to sit? I can pull up a chair?'

'Whatever feels comfortable.'

'You sure you've done this before?'

'I did life-drawing every week in college.'

That much was true. It was where she had seen her first in-the-flesh penis, apparently. Ms Driscoll did not have one of those. She had a body very different to the other life-drawing models. Saggier. Softer. Like mouldy fruit. If you pressed her, your finger might make a dent. It was easy to make things up when drawing. Leave the breast un-nippled, the vagina inoffensively cleftless. Photography was different. Ruder.

Ms Driscoll said nothing, but tied a bright paisley scarf around her skull, knotting it like a land-girl's. She stood anchored with a fist on each hips, and then pulled a chair out from underneath a dust-sheet. She placed it in the middle of the room, resting her elbows on the two ears of the chair, buttocks raised haughtily behind her.

At last, my mother looked up and took in her specimen obliquely. By staring directly at the white trunk of neck, she got to see the tops of what looked to be a heavy, garrulous pair of breasts. By examining the pale tundra of paunch, she got to see the top-corners of a vagina pinned by two hip bones. As a compromise, my mother focused her attention on Ms Driscoll's kneecaps. Kneecaps, to my mother's mind, were the least sexual part of the human body. If she stared at them too long, they turned into baby faces.

'Now, if you'd like to uncross your legs… not that far! Maybe turn them to the side a little? Then rest one hand on your right leg and the other on the chair?' She took a look through the eye of the camera. 'Perhaps try tilting your head? Did you want to smile, or?'

Ms Driscoll, folding her arms, looked down the barrel of the lens.

'Be honest.'

My mother pulled her eye from the shutter.

'You've never done this before.'

My mother turned a cardinal red.

'No.'

You would be hard pressed to call her a prude, my mother. She was young and newly out of college and liked to think herself experimental. She knew that there were reasons for naked bodies, as everybody did. They were for looking at, or for washing, or for being spread out on the pages of magazines. She knew there was a point to what Ms Driscoll was asking her to do but it was probably a point that only Ms Driscoll knew about. My mother, who was just following orders, didn't know why a fat dying woman would want to be photographed naked. Fat and dying was one thing. Naked was another.

'Well?' asked Ms Driscoll. 'How would you sit?'

'I'm sorry?'

'How would you sit if you were me?'

My mother thought about this and walked up to the seat, rearranging Ms Driscoll like a shop mannequin. Legs and arms straight-jacketed across each other. Buttocks and breasts reigned in, suggestionless. Not a flap of the darker flesh of the body exposed. She might as well have been wearing a bathing suit. Ms Driscoll sighed.

'For God's sakes. Get undressed, have a play around. I'll go downstairs. There's a mirror in the far-corner if you need to get your bearings.'

With that she walked out of the attic-room and back down the stairs. Her housecoat was still on the floor.

'Radiotherapy,' Ms Driscoll called out after herself. 'Makes you do mad things…'

***

It took them just one hour out of the guaranteed twenty four. They decided on three poses in the end. Sleeping lioness; Mary Magdalene (Ms Driscoll's working title) and Woman Straddling a Chair. Ms Driscoll acted and my mother directed. When they were both happy, or at least happier, they dressed again with their backs to each other and went downstairs. Ms Driscoll, a few steps ahead, was now holding the front door open for my mother.

'And who should I send them to?'

Ms Driscoll laughed. It was a tickled snicker which snowballed into a chuckle, then a cackle, then a howl. My mother stood on the doorstep and simpered patiently.

'Here! You send them straight back here! They're hardly for anyone else, are they? What could anyone else want with them?'

'I thought maybe...'

'Thought what?'

'Family or... friends, or something?'

That set off another avalanche.

'Imagine coming across *those* in a photo album!'

'Then... if it's not a rude question...'

'Oh, I'll hang them in my living room,' she said, 'so that every niece or nephew or brother or sister who turns up here knocking, wanting to know how I am, will get their answer.'

And Ms Driscoll closed the door on my mother and the rest of her story.

Bombay Mix and Pink Custard

Roshni Prasad

On the 7th September, much to the surprise and horror of Doncaster's Hindu Community, I moved into my grandparents' house with my white boyfriend. It was perhaps my most scandalous action since the Diwali raffle of 2011. Unfortunately, the issue of rents and deposits without a contract of employment had become insurmountable. Fortunately, my grandfather was quick to offer up our old family home as a temporary fix.

The previous tenant had been unceremoniously shifted two weeks ago. As we transferred our cardboard boxes into the large, stone house, my boyfriend (who was named Edmund, but consistently called Edward by my grandad, Thatha), mused on how he was surprised that the renter hadn't wanted to purchase the property.

'Yes, I hadn't expected him to,' Thatha replied. 'I think he is the kind of man who has no plans or ambition in life.' Ed's stifled laugh turned into a series of alarming coughs.

We were to stay in the master bedroom, and Thatha would come and go as he pleased, sleeping on a fold-away camp bed in the guest room. A new double bed had been purchased especially for us; quite the ground-breaking step from the family that also insisted that my mother have an arranged marriage, within her caste, twenty years ago. (Ed had once enquired about my caste, and upon hearing that it was comprised of cowherds, joked that he would be expecting a hefty dowry payment to compensate). There was no other furniture in the room, so we neatly arranged our sparse possessions in a pattern around the floor before returning to the car.

Thatha needed some more boxes, so he called up a contact to procure them. I was immediately certain that this was an Asian contact, as he began bellowing into the phone at twice the volume. He then disappeared upstairs, and returned carrying a printer in his arms, trying to peek around to navigate the slim hallways.

We opened the car boot, and the printer was haphazardly positioned within. Thatha drove out of the winding, tree-lined roads of our small estate, across the main road and into the neighbouring suburb. Young teenagers in tracksuit bottoms leapt out of the street, shooting mean glares from the pavement. Thatha muttered out loud the words that he read on street signs and shop fronts. The SUV parked up around the next corner, and Ed bolted into Coopland's, eager to snack on something that wasn't expired Bombay Mix.

A middle-aged Punjabi man emerged from the corner shop on the right, pausing to check on the awning that advertised cheap international calls with Lycamobile, and enthusiastically shook my grandfather's hand. They engaged in animated conversation before the corner shop proprietor approached my rolled-down window.

'This is your granddaughter?' he asked, whilst looking directly at me and nodding. I, too, nodded. 'Your grandad tells me that you can edit my daughter's personal statement. She wants to read Medicine at Trinity College.'

I nodded again, this time knowingly, and wondered which family member really wanted to read Medicine at Trinity College, and what chance she would stand against the public school students with their hours of tutoring. Thatha assured his acquaintance that I was indeed a Cambridge graduate, but didn't mention the 2:2. Ed returned with five packets of Chocolate Crunch and two tins of custard. 'I think your friend Rachel is in that sandwich shop.'

Rachel had, in fact, been a friend since our first days at primary school, and so I bounded over just as she exited the shop. Her hair was shorter, and she was five-months-pregnant. We were both equally startled at this encounter.

'I didn't know you were back,' she said, first. 'Not moving to London?'

'Maybe next year.' The failure to secure a job outside of Yorkshire had been a topic of repeated discussion. 'We just arrived today. You're having a baby!'

She glanced down, as though she had forgotten the bump was there. 'Not announced yet. I'll probably post the next ultrasound on Facebook. It's a boy.' That was why I hadn't known; it hadn't been on Facebook. With promises of catching up later, she took her leave.

'Congratulations!' I hurriedly called after her, feeling an uncomfortable mixture of jealousy and relief that I was not in her position.

'Let's get breakfast,' announced Thatha. Ed and I walked briskly after him.

The gentleman from the corner shop shouted, 'Thank you, Doctor!', before hauling his new printer into the store. Thatha dragged us to a greasy spoon that was not as expected. The clientele was all male, loud and bearded, and the table tops sticky. It didn't align with his lounge suit and good black shoes.

Despite these seemingly marked differences, he was getting on quite well with the construction workers who were enjoying a cuppa by the till; one of them even clapped him on the back when he offered them an extra hash-brown. Their expression towards Edmund, who had wrapped a pastel coloured sweater around his shoulders, was altogether more critical. 'I'm actually not that hungry, anymore,' Ed told me quietly, not averting his eyes from the other diners. We sat on the pavement outside and waited for Thatha to order a Full English to go.

The Chocolate Crunch wasn't quite the same school-dinner pudding without its signature pink custard, but I still appreciated that Edmund had remembered my favourite dish. He swept the cocoa crumbs away from our new bed sheets as I continued to eat.

'I have a surprise to show you,' he said. 'An activity.'

I rose onto my haunches, my interest piqued. 'What kind of activity?'

'A planning one.' He brandished a colourful world map from his backpack and straightened out the creases on the bed.

My eyes flitted between him and the map. 'You want to travel the world?'

'Do you want to stay in Doncaster?' he replied. This wasn't a question.

'I've never been out of Europe,' I told him. This was a reminder.

'We can start in Taiwan. I saw flights for £300.' He drew a red line in felt-tip, spanning from Manchester to Taiwan. It seemed rather a long way.

I stood up, paced to the bay window at the other side of the room. Three children on bikes lapped in circles around the cul-de-sac. Someone's mum leaned out of the window to shout that tea was ready.

'We should invite our friends round, throw a house party. It will be like sixth form again. The neighbours might even complain.'

'*Your* friends,' he corrected, absentmindedly, still engrossed in his map.

Thatha was more enthused at the prospect of the party. 'Is Maria going to be coming?' Maria was one of his favourites. 'She can use my bed,' he continued. 'I will go see your grandma at Ramesh Uncle's house.' My grandma was staying with her friend, Rekha Aunty, whilst Thatha searched for their down-sized home. They would spend all day shopping, gossiping, complaining about their husbands and singing praises about their grandchildren. Then, my grandma would return home and hurriedly throw salt in my face, to usher away any bad omens from the aforementioned bragging.

Ed arrived downstairs for dinner, just as the gentleman that had been repairing the boiler took his leave. 'Thank you very much, love,' Thatha called to him as he headed to his van.

'Does your grandad always call other men 'love'?' asked Ed.

I tutted in response. 'He doesn't conform to gender stereotypes.'

Thatha had collected a chicken curry from the Bangladeshi curry house down the road, who still included two extra *aloo tikkas* for me, 'on the house'. He served it up with a pack of flour tortillas, and Ed began to construct a fajita-style wrap.

'Do you like spicy food, Edward?' Thatha asked, scooping up a piece of chicken with his hand and raising it to his mouth. He received a suitably defensive-of-masculinity response.

The kids next-door were having a screaming match in the garden.

'They are quite loud, aren't they?' Ed commented.

'Sometimes it's good to have a bit of noise,' Thatha countered. 'Otherwise, you have to pinch yourself to remind you that you're alive.'

The lack of furniture might have been a problem, but an excess of bedding and cushions had instead transformed our once grand living room into a budget shisha lounge. Six litres of Strongbow cider and a multipack of Nik Naks from my grandad lay in wait on the coffee table; I hadn't the heart to tell him that three years at university had matured our tastes.

There had once been thirty of us school-friends, but now we were ten. The ones that remained were an eclectic mix, not familiar enough to fall easily back into place, with jarring cases of forced laughter and passing remarks that were lost in translation. We reminisced on terrorising P.E. teachers and clubbing at age sixteen, stories that Edmund hadn't collected in his seven years at a Surrey all-boys grammar school. His laughter was perhaps the most forced.

I wondered if this was actually a terrible idea. My sixth-form glory days could not be recreated, not with this group of people in this empty house. Half of them weren't drinking, and the other half were necking tequila. Half were discussing the offers they'd made on £80,000 houses on the slightly dodgier end of the high street, and the other half boasted their £40,000 starting salary in Slough. Suddenly, the home that I had grown up in and the people that I had grown up with felt like strangers.

Ed was in rapt conversation with my former classmate Tim, discussing the merits of London Business School's networking opportunities. 'Tim's graduate scheme has a secondment in South-East Asia,' he explained. 'You could do something like that, if you'd apply for banking! Don't you have family in Singapore?'

'I don't want to travel the world. I don't want a year in Singapore. I don't even want to move to London,' I confessed.

'What else would you do? Stay in Doncaster?' This was still not a question. I thought of Rachel, popping around for tea with her new baby boy. I thought of another weekend, trapped at home with Chocolate Crunch and custard, and nosy neighbours, and pushy Indian parents who wanted me to train their kids. I thought of a formal dinner at Cambridge, trapped inside my own reluctance to speak and fear of knowing too little. Why would all of that training and ambition end in silence at a formal?

I found Rachel, told her that I was jealous of her pregnancy, imagining how all-encompassing it would feel to grow and nurture a life. She shook her head. 'You're going to be a career woman, remember? You won't have a baby until you're twenty-eight. That's a good time.' It was settled, then. I would dwindle away the next seven years until my time arrived.

My grandad's penchant for cleaning came in handy the next day. I watched from our makeshift dining table, stealing the occasional glance outside. The paper of the 'For Sale' sign fluttered in the wind.

'How long do you think it will take to sell?' I asked. He knew, already, that I was asking how long I would have here.

'There's not much for you in Doncaster,' he replied. 'You are a girl with lots of plans and ambition. You didn't go to University to come back here.' He was already resigned, bracing himself for disappointment. But I was never one to disappoint.

'I know,' I mumbled. 'It's fun to think of, though.'

The house was sold two months later, to a family with three children and two dogs. My grandparents moved to be closer to my cousins. Edmund travelled the world, alone. I became a banker, and returned only to visit Rachel and her son, in her new home in my old neighbourhood, and thought wistfully of how I might have enjoyed life differently had I not had my personal statement edited by Rekha Aunty's clever, Oxford daughter.

Viaticum

Louie Broadhead

The problems began a full year prior to Father's departure.

By that time I had stopped going to St Thomas's, so I wasn't there to see the accusing looks or hear the muttered comments. Nor was I there to see him go, though technically no one was. It was September and he was spending his annual two weeks in Southport. At the end of the fortnight he didn't arrive back, though a message from the Bishop's Office did, explaining that Father Bernard had left unexpectedly due to extenuating personal circumstances; that a parish profile would be drawn up and a suitable replacement found... Of course, everybody knew that his sudden departure had everything to do with mine.

The doctors here say that it wasn't my fault, though I know different. My favourite is Dr Portman; he must be nearing my parents' age and is all teeth, hair, and jaw. The nurses act differently around him and I am conscious that I do too. Some people have that effect, good-looking people, intelligent people, they come to expect a certain level of deference. But you mustn't think I'm talking about Father. He wasn't like that.

The difficulty comes in trying to pin-point when exactly the problems began. I tried to entertain Dr Schultz, my psychiatrist, by telling her about school. About playing mass while everybody else would play kiss-catch, forcing my few friends (or 'followers') to act as congregants and sit obediently while I lectured them on sin. It annoyed me when the boys became restless and began comparing Yu-Gi-Oh cards, distracting me from my homily. At primary school, everybody played those cards. This was mass, however, so I decided to show them the prayer cards I carried in my coat pocket. One had picture of St. Catherine of Sienna on it, another instructed the reader that I was Catholic and they should contact a priest if I was dying. The boys thought I wanted to exchange them and laughed, which upset me, then they went on ignoring me and comparing power ratings. The mass truly over by this point, I explained to them that St. Catherine trumped all of their cards because she was the Spiritual Bride of Christ, that she wore his foreskin as a wedding ring...

They asked me what a foreskin was.

I said I didn't know.

Anyway, that was the first time that I felt it – the feeling of utter despair, the desire simply not to be – because after that the boys got sick of me and threw my cards in a puddle. I cried not because the colours bled or because the cards were still crinkled, even when I pressed them in my Bible, but because Father had given them to me. Those two were not my only cards, but they were my only ones from Father. In fact, my own collection was quite extensive. There were the obvious ones: St Thérèse of Lisieux, St Theresa of Avila, St Francis of Assisi (which, admittedly, I had chosen for the animals). Then there were some obscurer choices: levitating monks, medieval virgins. I particularly liked martyrs, those who had died brutal, bloody deaths: wheel and rack, burnings, copy-cat crucifixions. Father would tell me the stories of each one before mass, quoting from the particular saint's writings and Butler's *Lives*.

Remembering all of this, I got rather carried away and forgot that Dr Schultz was there.

When I paused she said, 'If my child were dying, I would want somebody to call the Emergency Services, not a priest.'

I told her Last Rites are a sort of emergency service, in a way. This was meant to be funny.

She did not smile.

All of that had been when I was younger though. The real problems had begun with the misunderstanding about the candle. As lead altar server it was my job to put the candles out after mass. We had a long brass instrument for this purpose, which meant I could reach the tall candles on the altar and side altar without help. Putting the candles out one Sunday, the hot metal caught my hand and left a nasty burn. It hurt, but Father's reaction hurt more. He said that we didn't want any more accidents of that kind and maybe it would be best for him to put the candles out himself from now on. Only when I got home did Mum and Dad suggest that maybe I shouldn't be serving anymore.

'Fifteen is a little bit old, sweetie' said Mum. 'Besides, you'll have your exams soon. You don't want too many commitments.'

They were smiling but I could tell they didn't believe what they were saying. Serving was my only commitment. It was Father speaking, not them.

***

The first time that I sinned I did not understand what was happening, though I cried afterwards – not only for what I had done, but for what it made me. I was on the floor in my room, praying to be made a server again. There was an image taped on my wardrobe door, a painting of St. Sebastian given to me by a woman from church. The woman was a widow and wore an ostentatious black mantilla. She had bought the picture for me in Rome, because Sebastian is the saint after whom I am named. My eyes focused on the saint while I prayed: eyes glancing Heaven-ward, mouth agape in prayer. His arrow-punctured chest was creased in agony, making his loin cloth buckle suggestively at the groin.

That was when it happened. The rhythm of my rocking back and forth in time to the rosary, the rub of my trousers against my leg – broken suddenly by a leap in my pulse, the turning tide in the pit of my stomach. At first I thought that this was a religious ecstasy, like St. Theresa in *The Interior Castle*. Only afterwards did I understand, laid on the floor, whispering empty prayers into the carpet and weeping, while my breathing returned to normal and the warmth spread in my pants.

I confessed it, of course; crying again in the confessional when I had to re-tell the story and begging the forgiveness of God. If Father had thought that I was not careful enough to be a server, then he would know now that I was not good enough either. Instead, he explained to me delicately that there had been no intent and technically what I had done wasn't a sin, that there was no penance necessary and moreover such things could happen to boys my age…I shouldn't be too hard on myself. The words consoled me at the time, though later I chastised myself for crying so openly and thus cheating myself out of forgiveness. Clearly he had not understood.

It was for this reason that I decided to give myself my own penance. This involved praying the rosary and long, complicated novenas, or reciting the Litany of the Saints late into the night. I did this for a few weeks, during which time I slept very little. My parents were still in the habit of looking in on me to check if I was asleep, so I would lie in bed with my back to the door until they left, then spend the rest of the night on the floor. Normally I managed to last until dawn, when I would climb back into bed and doze for a few hours before school. That final Sunday morning, however, I woke up on the floor to find that it had happened again during the night.

That was when I knew that I was evil.

I thought about saying that I was ill and wanted to stay at home, that I had lots of homework to do – anything to avoid the stigma of not receiving communion. How easily my tongue now turned to lies and deceit. To make things worse, when I got to church, none of the other servers had turned up. Father asked me if I would stand in. Under any other circumstances I would have been delighted about this, but now sitting right at the front would only make my shame even more noticeable.

I went into the sacristy to get my albs and found one of the church's handymen installing a new shelf. A chunk of plaster had come out with the old fitting, so he was letting the filler set during the service. The shelf, his screws, and his screwdriver were set out on the floor.

Mass went well until the Communion Rite. Father approached me as normal with the host and I ducked my head. This was made even more mortifying because he didn't understand I was refusing and all but forced the bread onto my lips, which remained firmly closed. My parents sat shame-faced in the front pew and the rest of the congregation began whispering audibly. My face flushed and I began to sweat.

When the mass was over I went back into the sacristy. The sound of the congregation talking in the porch (no doubt about me) seemed distant here, and for some privacy I latched the door.

The idea did not come to me immediately. Just like the time with the candle – holding my hand to the flame until my flesh blistered and bled, until Father had interrupted me and I made it look like an accident – now I acted as if in a trance.

The handle was tried and then there was a knock at the door, Father's voice saying my name consolingly. A few more knocks and then a rising intonation, a more determined try of the handle. I cannot remember at exactly what point the other voices joined his, only that the knocking turned to banging at the sound of the screwdriver, as if they were trying to force the door.

Inside, I genuflected towards a crucifix on the wall, crossed myself calmly and positioned the screw in the centre of my palm…

***

Dr Portman is a nice man. Perhaps I shall be a doctor, given that I think I can no longer be a priest. He told me that I will always have the scar, the circle of pink, lacerated flesh at the centre of my palm the size of a penny. Oddly, I am quite grateful for this. Sometimes in the night, when my thoughts are most troubling, I trace its contours, fingering the sudden smoothness in the centre of my life-line for reassurance.

I wasn't out of hospital when Father left, but I was there to watch the moving van arrive outside of the clergy house. None of the other parishioners were there, though I thought that maybe Father might come and not tell anybody. Apparently he did not leave his house for days after the ambulance took me away; he was quite distraught. I wanted to tell him not to blame himself, that it wasn't his fault. Instead, the removal men picked up the keys from the parish office and began emptying the contents of Father's house into the back of the van. He didn't have many belongings, really. Most of the furniture was owned by the Church. It seemed a shame I had no gift to give him, seen as I was the one who had made him leave.

The van was white, but the back of it was dirty and in the dirt people had scrawled obscenities and crude phalluses, drawn their names and those of others with hearts around them.

This seemed vulgar to me, so I went up and drew a cross with two fingers, pressing down hard and retracing the two lines over and over again until it was pure white against the dusty grey-brown. I imagined Father, wherever he was, seeing the cross and smiling, wondering who had drawn it, and so – even if he did not know it – thinking of me.

Two for Joy by Rebecca Sillis

Before the Bullet

Millie Guille

before the bullet washed through your heart, like rain. Do you. Remember. My ankles, swollen body. i sat in your arms and laughed. Baby-book twisted at the spine. Gael's hiccups warm against your hand, through my skin. Before the bullet you were. Beautiful. Do i remember. Soft eyes maple mouth. Straight teeth, those white teeth we prayed he'd have. The eggs i cracked that morning on the floor. Their absence in the cool-box. You wrote HUEVOS in capitals and went to get them. That quick kiss that cross kiss you threw against my head. Before the. Bullet you were shouting, at the radio the soccer its tinny ads. You were singing and i felt him. Swirling. Eight-months strong, needing to get to. You. He's been needing to get. To you for thirteen years is a long time without your. Breath. On my breasts i'm waiting for your face at the door. Before. The bullet washed through, your heart like rain

on a thursday afternoon

Sarah Collins

I'm here
wrapped in a duvet
that like the clothes
in the basket
begs for the washing machine
and his drumming spin.
the sink and toothbrush
are achingly far,
with every hour they
seem to drift a few feet backwards
as the sulking clouds
gather, abandoning their play.
late afternoon is a voyeur,
inching back the curtains
lingering at the door,
It came for me then and
with hand upon my shoulder
coaxed me back beneath the covers
with false promises and
weighted bargains.

Freewheelin'

Tom Walden

As the bucket is plunged, empty, down and outs gather towards the harbourside, tattooed men
advise where to go next – "By them grockles; reeling it in, they were."

Their pint glasses line the walls, and she sets the Echo board, swells intense
already with the day. Advance
onto broken plains; long spray, exalts flashing, the wake ends.

Our scampers offer little, points catching every time. A glance –
they cling. Stolid, now and again
a pebble's needed to prise them off. We rise and wait, they loosen, calm;

So I bash, and he retrieves. H.B. – "I'll give you that, and hook them."
"Stinks; but fine, you next time."
Our knees scuff, against and together, we pull – until at last, white concrete defends.

Up on the front, pastel-coloured homes obscure the sky; blinds
open, doors drawn, their motion
keenly returns, and holidaymakers haul past the dulcet signs;

Careering, wooden horses grind along the eye. No devotion
in this town, his pleading son;
stood between, the ocean recedes – in falls a drunk, overdone.

Out of Season

Joy Hunter

Our watering can filled quickly to the brim,
Bellowing silver from the garden tap
You went over to the trees, picked out a perfect apple
And you smiled as I crunched away at it.

But it was the wrong season for apples, surely
And we never lived near an orchard –
Perhaps some imagined memory has been stirred up
From the stem of not remembering, from the pain –
As I wonder down the suburbs of Appleyard's Lane

This bit I'm sure of.
You told me that if I ate all the pips
A tree would grow out slowly from my stomach
I cried that night in bed- I was that scared
(And I want to remember you hearing and coming in)
But the tree never came
And now all the seasons have changed –

Because losing you that young was just too much
Or was it? It was
An over-flowing watering can
An apple, too big for small hands
And I never really knew you- I can't remember –
Instead I'm told this and that
And given back my stunted roots in whispers

And so the grief grows up with you, don't you see
Deeply rooted, like a black seed, or a tumour
A pip you can't spit out

Ithaca

William Hosie

you fumble your way out of bed
to see Dawn's red clouds bleed
onto the Ionian Sea
onto the balcony
the morning breeze blows memories from the night before
cigarette butts, tea leaves, poetic scribbles on paper sheets
rustling against your feet
curling back inside, you draw the curtains
to soften the tango light that flutters as they sway
gracefully they dance and their bodies collide
drawn together by fragility
the clouds are swept away as you fall back to sleep
somnolent smiles dreaming up
your little odysseys

Westeast

Alice Yu Frederick

When we were so little our teeth
were deciduous, my white cousin made
his first racist joke, stretching his eyes
into slits. Uncontrolled

snickers & tears gurgled from my face
which back then had fewer holes,
no pearlgaps, no open pores.
It might have eased the pressure,

having taller nostrils or wider laugheyes
than my curvesquints, but my humor
& horror popped, leaked,
crashing past the membrane

of my cheeks. I fractured
like a moonjar, one shard
of me his yellow mask, the other
a mottled glaze underneath.

Self-Portrait by Sophie Hardcastle

In Chiapas, Subcommandante Marcos of the EZLN Describes what Hope is

Sam Dunnett

"A flower, yes, that flower of hope."
What does he mean by "yes",
that sower of weightless seeds?
What right does he have to make a word a thing?
Yes, the smell of buttered toast was carried
over the black ridges of Catalonian trenches
to speak utopia to stomachs.
Yes, at times like these,
a conversation about trees is almost
a crime, as Brecht wrote almost
correctly. Yes, we move sideways, backwards,
sometimes almost
forwards. Yes, we mean that we speak in things,
and the things we speak of
happened. Yes, there's something else
to speak of. Always, yes, always.

Slivers

Paige Pinto

On New Year's Eve, a man clasps my hand over the shaft of a chef's knife and shows me how to decapitate a bottle of champagne. Ichor spills out frothy, and I catch it in crystal flutes and pass it round. I slashed open the back of my bodice with a pair of sewing shears while dressing, and now *he* is running his fingers up and down my spine, precarious and hot as breath.

I do the next three bottles, wielding the knife like a sword, pressing it flush against each bottleneck. Arms strong, diaphragm tight, slice through glass on an exhale.

Three-thirty in the morning, I step out from a cab alone, and cold salt air sucks the moisture from my mouth, the memory of his caress in the guest bathroom from my skin. I want to do it again. Inside, parched raw, I shuck my parka, and the split dress flutters half-heartedly, like broken wings. In the hall mirror, my spine juts out at hard angles, a cliff edge from the gaping expanse of my back.

I need lemons.

There are seven in a ceramic bowl with a scalloped edge on top of the refrigerator; I bought it a month ago to cheer the place up. Now I pluck it down. The lemons look okay, oblong and dimpled and green in places, but no mould. I tip the bowl and let them loose on the floor. They rollick into constellation.

I draw my own chef's knife from the block by the sink and consider the riddle. Squat on haunches, corral three lemons, choose one. I trace the blade in a straight line from navel to navel, pressing the fruit close in with my palm.

I even close my eyes, so that for a moment I am still there, with the small of my back pressed close in against the corner of the towel rail, my head wrenched to the side like a dead bird in ecstasy; I am there until the blade breaks through the rind and blooms red against my hand.

I carve the lemon into wedges and one at a time place them between my teeth.

Bite. Suck.

Citric acid fizzes. The space behind my eyes shocks alive, and deep in my belly a trickle, like blood beginning to flow. My gums swell and blister; my teeth root and file into fangs.

Again –

I fall upon the rest of the lemons, hacking them into constituent parts, knife scratching at wood-look linoleum, until juice leaches into small puddles and my feet and arms are stinging with pulp.

I slurp up a segment with my lips kissing the floor.

trial 6

Ella Blackburn

My mum keeps all of our smashed mugs.

I must try very hard not to touch you. Or, when I do, it must be precise. To touch you has a different weight to when I touch others. With everyone else, I can slide slightly out of place, or misjudge a step and bump, or knock my chin too hard onto their temple as I balance my head on theirs. But with you, I am careful. I am delicate. When you rest your shoulders on my chest, I can feel the bones in your back and the blood rush under your skin. I must hold completely still, so that you stay just as you are. I watch my breath gently shake your hair. I must be perfect, I must be precise. I am holding the most beautiful bubble in my hands, and I must not break it. I hazard a tap here on your hip. Yes, that was safe. Perhaps a touch here behind your ear? No, I must be cautious. Gently, ever so gently, I lower my gaze and look from your cheek to the bridge of your nose. The light is shining through your eye. My chest is a paper fan opening. My chest is a hair clip closing. Your body relaxes. You sink further into my lap. It is almost unbearable. And yet, you are sufferable.

free object

Emily Fitzell

here
    in your abstract terms
    our equivalences fold

        and i forget myself

        stripped to
        our vectors

    we move
    just as cubic rhythms
    of mass

move our memories of
the faithful and the finite

    they say other types of
    forgetfulness
    give rise to

    objects

    like
    free
    objects

Grey Street by Matthew Seccombe

memorial ii

Michelle Angwenyi

These are the elaborate one-sided goodbyes.
Learning to accept tea from strangers.
The voiceless convergence of winds.
——
A child half-known,
Their distance half-known
——
Escaping the lovers of plants,
Tender, soft-hearted, soft-footed
Their lone walks in museums,
the whisperings among fossils.
——
Their dedication to water,
against sound.
The inhabitance of pale yellow;
——
The slowness of arrival. The always arriving.
The day, and its salt pillars.
And the sun, still water.

Hello, Nightline

Roshni Prasad

Moira had been hoping that the telephone wouldn't ring. *Resent* was a strong word, and one entirely inappropriate for her vocabulary this evening, but she could not deny the heavier feeling in her chest upon hearing its shrill calls.

Her bedfellow blinked at her from the sofa. 'Do you want me to-' she began in a hoarse voice, rising onto her elbows. Moira hurriedly assured her that this would not be necessary, and swung to her feet, towards the adjoining room. The cold was always the worst, and she had just made a fresh cup of Earl Grey, which now lay in wait on the kitchen counter.

'Hello, Nightline,' she welcomed in her usual tone, not too bright and not too flat, whilst settling into the desk chair. It sounded as though the caller were outdoors as the wind rustled through the handset, and their heavy breathing suggested that they might be walking rather quickly. She pre-empted a request for taxi numbers and began to reach for the file that contained them.

'I'm not depressed,' came a deep voice, probably male. Moira dropped the file and leaned back into her seat.

'Okay,' she replied.

'Don't do the thing where you just keep saying 'okay'. I'll hang up if you do.' His tone was simultaneously threatening and calm. Moira remained unfazed.

'I'll try not to,' she appeased, in what she hoped was a compromising manner. She hadn't realised how often she relied on facial expressions to gauge situations, prior to this, and felt that she had lost an important sense. Staring at the blank, yellow wall opposite was unhelpful.

'Sorry. I don't mean to be combative.'

'How has your day been?'

'It's fucking cold. I thought the south was warm?' She recognised a Scottish lilt in his voice.

'Well, it is January. And it's two A.M.'

'That was judgy. You aren't allowed to pass judgments, are you?'

'No. Just stating a fact.' She tried to remain confident, although the usual Moira would have immediately apologised. Nightline Moira didn't apologise unless she'd made a mistake, and that had not yet occurred.

'I wish I weren't here right now. University towns are the worst kind of drab.'

'Where would you prefer to be?' Moira asked.

He hummed in thought. 'Somewhere snowy and crisp.'

'Didn't you just complain about the cold?'

'I don't like the cold when it is not meant to be cold,' he clarified, with a sigh. 'Places that are covered in dramatic peaks of snow and ice are just made for such weather. And I admire that.'

'It does sound peaceful,' she agreed.

'If you could return to somewhere you'd visited, where would it be? I've just put £500 into your hands. Highly generous, I know.'

She wasn't supposed to talk about herself.

'Morocco.' It had been wondrous. 'The colours, the smells, standing at the foot of a waterfall at the top of the Atlas Mountains and feeling the magnitude of your hiking achievement.'

'You're quite the poet.'

'I do try.'

'I suspected so. Will you read me an actual poem of yours?'

She was flattered.

'Of mine? Absolutely not.'

'Well. Poetry is boring, anyway.' A sudden mood change. She heard a door slam in the background, then less noise altogether.

She let the silence sit, and he filled it.

'It's been a rough week.'

'How so?'

'Too many endings. Not enough beginnings.'

'That *is* rough.'

'There's nothing worse than standing still.'

She considered this. 'Maybe it gives you time to look around?'

'Nothing worth looking at. It's all an iteration of something I've seen before.'

'Then start moving. You have some control.'

She should not have been advising him so directly.

'You raise an interesting point.'

He was pleased, again.

'What do you look like?' he paused. Somehow, although she could not see him, Moira recognised that this was a pause. 'I don't mean that in a creepy way. I mean in it in a… I feel that this might be an important conversation.'

'I'm not sure it matters. The conversation will still be important,' she replied.

'You're right. But if I've imagined you completely wrong, I won't have done you justice.'

'I fear that any description would compromise my anonymity.'

'Perhaps we have met,' he mused, and she heard the slosh of some liquid in a mug, somewhere in the background.

'I don't get out much,' Moira replied. She wanted to end such musings.

'My name begins with 'Y'. So, you could just call me 'Y'.'

'Why would I do that?'

'I see what you did there.' She heard the smirk tug at his lips.

'I don't know any 'Y's.'

'Probably a good thing. Now, tell me, why *did* your relationship fail?'

She pretended that the question hadn't startled her, and that it wasn't the very question playing across her mind for the past two months. 'To what relationship are you referring?'

'A romantic one, of course. I don't want to hear about your falling-out with your high-maintenance friends from Cheltenham Girls'.'

'Maybe they are the same thing.'

He sighed. 'Well, now I feel like a lousy heteronormative.'

'So you should. Why don't you answer the question first?' This was, after all, what he had intended from the start.

'It would appear,' he began, accompanied with more shuffling from the background, 'that I am an inherently selfish being. Although this is not an unusual feature, it is apparently undesirable.'

'It's not uncommon. Perhaps you will find someone more accommodating.' Moira realised that instilling hope was, ironically, not a skill she readily possessed.

'I plan on using this particular quality to my advantage. Selfish people can generate some satisfying outcomes.'

'How has it worked for you so far?'

'She was a real bitch, anyway. I shouldn't be blamed.'

'Blamed?'

'Not for what happened before, or for what happens next.'

'How were things before?'

'I don't care about the before. I'm looking for a beginning, but people are getting in the way.'

'How so?'

'She is getting in the way. It's time to take her out of the equation. Some people might be sad, of course, but it's better for everyone in the long run. She isn't contributing anything to the world.'

Things were getting odd.

'I just believe that society might have a warped view on the topic, is all. It shouldn't be seen as a crime. More of a favour.'

She tried to hold the phone steady, and swallow the lump growing up her throat. 'I'm going to hang up now.'

'Are you sure, Moira?'

She blinked at the receiver.

'Yes, I know it's you,' he continued. 'Consider your anonymity compromised. It was far too easy to urge you to confirm those specific details.'

Moira realised that the pool of Irish lesbians at her university was perhaps smaller than anticipated.

'I also happen to know where your office is.' He spoke casually, although merely referencing an off-hand comment about the weather. 'That's not information you would want in my hands, is it?'

She ran over the office's security system in her head, and decided that she was relatively safe, but the proximity to the riverbank was somewhat concerning. Hanging up no longer seemed appropriate.

He laughed, and the crackling that ensued offended Moira's eardrum.

'You're in some trouble now, aren't you? What protocol will you follow?'

She wondered if her partner had locked the door as she left. The hand clutching the phone had become uncomfortably damp.

'I'm going to end the call,' she decided.

'Do it. It's what you do afterwards that matters more.'

She realised she was holding her breath.

'Will you share what you know, knowing that I am entirely aware of your identity, and you are ignorant of mine? Or will you forget it ever happened, abscond responsibility and hope you don't read anything in next week's papers?'

He was bluffing. Maybe.

'I'm now going to end the call. This service is intended for genuine users, and you are occupying valuable time on our line.'

She should've hung up immediately.

'Do pass my regards onto whoever takes your place tomorrow night. I look forward to knowing them.'

Sonnet 1

Timothy Trayhurn

Indoctrination served to comfort me,
I walked in Christian armour's loose embrace
Under a lofty not-considered face,
I, a precocious child, enveloped warmly,
Saw fit to sin openly, wantonly,
Supposing He would try lightly my case,
Surely, for childhood's boon is limitless grace,
And I was loved, happy because He made me.
Perspective, however, uneasily rests
On fulcrums bound to careless circumstance.
Fleeting respite, from cruel and tragic chance,
A loved one found between welcoming breasts.
And now not having passed His c'lestial tests
She prances the screaming, naked, horror dance.

Prayer in Retrospect

Margaret Jones

Let it be waiting without expectancy.
Bone-blue skies that do not snow
A glass sitting empty by the sink

Let it be clear suddenly, be productive.
The painter's inspiration
The momentary heartsink of recognition
A polished mirror, the last page

Let it be the interruption.
The pricked balloon
First conversations
A call with news of a body

Let it be wound-healing.
Rain-soaked runs
A reluctant email
Side dishes passed at the dinner table

Let it be the immanence
A resolving chord,
Snowflakes under lamppost light

Bedside Intimacies by Freya Doggett

A Narrow Revolution

Annalisa Hoadley

Boat life on Regent's Canal

Things axed – upshot of her best-before-date;
ridding one's mask to live six feet by forty
(a perversion embargo). Tanks' mandate:
no hose no water, mine: piss in a pan
or risk overflow of__ handle it.
Aphrodite rules my willowed view, but this
Regent's too young for demigods or myth
– the coal catch silenced by its own Oily-puss.
Imputed by tripper cruises, *to the left*
the zoo – oh that's me. Data revolution:
my small home on your selfie-stick,
get that close you might drown (as well).
                    What's that smell? God;
black boat, black apron, black gold and suction!
Peter the Pump-Out. Saint. Happiest sod alive.

Medusa by Rebecca Sillis

Push_Pull

Amadeus Harte

As the coach pulled on to the dual carriageway and the fluorescent overhead lights dimmed, Zayneb felt her stomach relax. *The World Is Yours*, Nas assured through her headphones as she watched black trees race by a violet dusk. Being London bound always made her feel like she was shedding a seasonal artificial skin. No more having to grit her teeth as nearby Tories discussed the virtues of poverty at formal hall. Back to voluptuous laughter and legs dangling over the skate bowl in Meanwhile Gardens, chewing on jerk through the barbeque smoke with Deanna.

After the coach pulled in at Victoria, Zayneb made her way through the London tube maze, eventually emerging at Oval. Busses and cars motored down the Brixton Road past William Hill and Dallas Chicken House. She caught sight of her reflection in a pub window, dimly illuminated by the glow of a pink neon light proclaiming *Good Vibes Only*. She assessed whether she should have straightened her afro, compulsively sprucing at the dark curls framing her cheeks. Why should I be compelled to ruminate over my appearance at every opportunity that presents itself to me, she thought as she strode towards Cable Cafe.

She was 30 minutes early to interview an artist named simply 'Frank'. Art magazines with smooth matte pages listed him as *simmering hot* after his debut at the Whitechapel Gallery and she figured she had nothing to lose by sending his Facebook page a message with an interview request. He accepted, and even went as far as to like her profile photo, which she acknowledged was a serious score in itself. She pitched the interview to an established indie culture mag who gave her the green light, her first paid piece. There was no possibility for Zayneb to commit even the slightest of errors in the face of such an opportunity.

Cable Cafe was unassuming, situated between Lucky Day Chinese Takeaway and Your Choice Convenience Store. She entered under a green and white striped awning and assumed residence at the bar. 'Just a coffee for now thanks', she told the bartender, a young, gentle mannered white man with a thin paisley scarf draped around his shoulders. He began whirring up the coffee grinder over the lull of dreampop music which Zayneb considered mild and didn't connect with. It was a quaint and pared back venue with spider plants pouring over makeshift bookshelves on tattered persian rugs. Cafe by day, bar by night. Upturned bowl shaped lamps hung from the ceiling like UFOs, giving the room a buttery glow. Outside, it started to drizzle.

She had already prepared a list of questions to ask Frank, but she knew she'd probe each of his answers with novel ones. Zayneb was sharp and fully intended to broach difficult topics. Yet she also knew she needed to get him on her side without presenting as a fluttering fangirl. This was priority number one. 24 year old Frank had started out as an untrained artist widely regarded as 'political' or socially transgressive. His work consisted of looming, hyperrealist paintings of corporate elites in compromised positions. Steve Jobs in a sweatshop or Uber executives in the dole queue under the banner: *Disruptive Innovation*. He'd sell the pieces on the street outside the Goldman Sachs headquarters on Fleet Street until the bizzies moved him along. He was remarkably prolific and topical, poking fun at whatever characters public media opinion decided were unsavory. A freelancer for *Raw Art* profiled him, and soon after publication, an anonymous benefactor commissioned a portrait of Harvey Weinstein. He was to present the piece outside Weinstein's home in LA. Within two weeks, *#MeToo* was unveiled to a smirking, shades clad crowd. It depicted the predator sprawled on a film set; lights searing into meaty flesh, being pawed at triumphantly by a group of female Hollywood stars. The piece was put up for auction, the winning bid being $50k.

As she sat at the bar, Zayneb was highly aware of her body language. She positioned herself strictly upright and surveyed the menu so that she'd know exactly what to order by the time Frank arrived. As much contempt as she had for *Lean In*, she endeavoured to hold herself in a way that was not overtly dainty, no crossed hands or legs. The nerves were starting to creep through her gut and she allowed herself to indulge a nervous tic, rapid left foot shaking, until she saw Frank approach through the window. She hoovered in a lungful of air and slid off the bar seat as he entered Cable Cafe.

'Frank! Thanks so much for coming, man.'

He approached her and went in for a hug, but she extended her hand with a confident smile. 'Ah, where are my manners?' he said in a rare cockney drawl, laughing, slapping his free hand over hers. He was tall and broad, over 6' and chiselled, with dark hair and chocolate eyes. He had a snug silver hoop in one of his earlobes and sported an exclusively black outfit. Zayneb gestured for him to take a seat at the bar.

'Beer? On me.' she said. He raised an eyebrow jokingly and ordered the house wheat whilst Zayneb ordered a Merlot.

'So it's been an interesting few months for you,' she began. 'You've gone from being a vanguard street vendor to an artworld darling in a matter of months.' She produced her phone from her pocket and showed Frank that she was pressing the record button before placing it on the bar.

Frank nodded continuously 'Yeah, it's been a bit mad,' he answered, and they ping-ponged back and forth about the highs and lows of fame and how it's not all it's cracked up to be, you never know who to trust, it can be lonely, you can't forget your roots, etc. Zayneb sensed that Frank felt a natural affinity with her and they spoke as if they'd known each other for much longer than 10 minutes.

He detailed how his first auction had felt like being in the belly of the beast. 'So does that mean you're now one of the beasts?' asked Zayneb, smiling, looking up at him under thick lashes. The kind of people who could afford Frank's work were the kind of people who could easily rub shoulders with the subjects he depicted.

'No, the beasts just pay my rent,' Frank replied, running his hand through his hair. 'Anyone who's grown up on the dole knows what the first big paycheck feels like. You know Conor McGregor called his first yacht the 188 cause that's how much his dole was? Legend! It feels like being born.'

'So do you want to make money, or do you want to make art?' she asked, 'or is there a even a difference between the two anymore?'

He told her there wasn't, and at every point in human history and across all cultures, art has been exchanged as a commodity. Increasing numbers of bodies appeared around them in the cafe, and a waitress removed a nearby table so that a band of men with brass instruments could arrange themselves appropriately. A steamy fog crept up the windows.

'Does the current market value of your pieces change what they're trying to say? Actually, what *are* your pieces trying to say?'

'Interpretation lies in the eye of the beholder,' he answered defensively, swirling around the remains of his beer, letting himself off the hook. 'I just paint what I feel like painting. I don't like what the bankers did to our country during the crash, you know? Left my old man without a job.'

Zayneb intuited that the affinity between them was likely to dissolve if she continued with this line of questioning. She was well versed in the survivalist skill of disarming men whilst continuing to let them think they were in the driver's seat. She swiftly ordered another Merlot, knowing he would have to follow her lead, and offered a self-deprecating quip about the time she spilled red on the white silk blouse of her ex boyfriend's mother on their first meeting. Frank cringed and tut-tut-tutted through a grin. She laughed with him, at herself, and the band began to play. They clinked glasses.

They swivelled their stools around to face the band. Neither of them were expecting music tonight. After a few bars, she offered that the musicians were clearly technically skilled, yet something about the music felt forced. 'There's no swing. I can't explain it.'

'You're into jazz?' Frank inquired with candid enthusiasm, and they began exchanging their favourite artists and albums.

'I think for Mingus, jazz was about sex, like his stuff sounds kind of stormy with such swagger,' said Zayneb. When she spoke, her eyes lit up and she gesticulated vigorously against the glow of recently introduced candle light.

'You know he said that jazz men were sex slaves for the music industry?' Frank asked, leaning over the bar towards her, safeguarded by the convenient pretence of loud music.

She gulped her wine and told him what she wouldn't do to have seen Charlie M rip up a sweaty 60s club.

They spent the next half hour laughing and whooping over the agile bassline. They were on drink number 3 and shot number 1 and the recording phone had disappeared from the bar. More and more people began to occupy the venue as the air grew thick. Zayneb removed her pullover, revealing long, caramel arms either side of a navy silk blouse.

Frank brushed his hand against Zayneb's thigh in a manner which was intended to initially appear like an accident, but then it stayed there, as if the accident was a mutually welcomed occurrence. But it wasn't (is it ever?), and she felt that familiar swoop in the pit of her stomach when she knew it would be too awkward to actually draw attention to the fact that she was not enjoying male sexual entitlement. Does any woman? Frank continued talking about how artists and musicians were essentially the same kind of people, not like everyone else, while Zayneb was silently seething over the fact that men had the power to blunt her sharpness, producing her as something she wasn't. Fuck this, she thought, waves of disappointment crashing in her gut. He took her silence as an invitation for further intrusion, inserting his knee between her thighs.

'Let's get out of here, yeah?' he dictated, his nose inches from hers. She could feel his breath on her cheek and it made her face turn sour.

Zayneb entered flight mode. 'I have to catch the last coach home,' she said as she picked up the drinks menu from the bar and removed the phone underneath, pressing 'stop' with her thumb. She looked him directly in the eyes.

'Thanks for the interview, I'll send you the transcript when it's done,' she said in a forced tone, feeling her heartbeat in her throat. She slung her pullover over her arm and ignored Frank's predictable audacious protests insinuating her unreasonability.

Zayneb exited Cable Cafe and power walked towards the tube station, ensuring that she didn't look backwards. Experiences like these weren't new for her, yet despite their jarring frequency, she never grew accustomed to having the rug slowly pulled out from under her feet. The drizzle outside had matured into warm rain, and a glowing bus stop advertised shelter among other products and services. Her hands needed purpose, and regardless of the fact that she had recently given up smoking, she requested a cigarette from a teenage boy absorbed in his screen. He silently obliged, barely looking up. She took out her phone and began typing an email to her assigned editor using a single thumb with dexterous millennial speed. After she hit send, she resumed her journey back to Victoria Coach Station. She exhaled deeply and knew life would continue like it always does: push, pull, push, pull.

Contributor Notes

HARRI ADAMS is a third-year English Language and Literature student at Regent's Park College, Oxford and a former student of Caerleon Comprehensive School. His poetry has appeared in The ISIS and Ash. He can be contacted at hadams2011@hotmail.co.uk.

THEO AKIYAMA is a former joiner and woodworker, and current DPhil candidate in Theology at Oxford (Balliol). He can be contacted at theo.akiyama@gmail.com.

MICHELLE ANGWENYI is a Zoology student at Wolfson College, Cambridge, and has been shortlisted for the 2018 Brunel International African Poetry Prize. You can find more of her work at www.notjustwiththelions.wordpress.com.

ELLA BLACKBURN is a 1st-year Historian at St Catharine's College, Cambridge. She hopes to continue writing and making the most of all of Cambridge's writing opportunities. If you want to see more of her work, email her at ellablackburn@aol.com

LOUIE BROADHEAD is a second-year undergraduate studying English Language and Literature at Magdalen College, Oxford. He lives in the East Riding of Yorkshire and is currently completing his first novel.

OLIVER CANESSA is a final-year undergraduate reading Psychological and Behavioural Sciences at Corpus Christi College, Cambridge. He is a 'Renaissance man from Gibraltar.' www.olivercanessa.com

ROHIT CHAKRABORTY is reading for an MSt in World Literatures in English at St Edmund Hall, Oxford.

CHARLOTTE CLARK is a 4th-year student of French and Italian at King's College, Cambridge. She has a foundation diploma in fine art and has completed an apprenticeship in printmaking. Upon graduating she intends to develop her artistic practice further.

MARY ANNE CLARK is reading for an MSt in English at Merton College, Oxford. Her poems have appeared in The Mays, The Kindling, Oxford Poetry, IRIS III, and several Emma Press anthologies. She won the Newdigate Prize in 2016.

SARAH COLLINS is a final year Law student at Fitzwilliam College, Cambridge. She regularly performs spoken word poetry at the ADC 'Speakeasy' Nights and is a poetry editor for The Cambridge Pamphlet 2018. Her prose, journalism and poetry can be found at www.sarahcollinswrites.wordpress.com

LEV CROFTS is a first-year Archaeology and Anthropology student at St John's College, Oxford. He is currently the Fiction Director of *The Isis* Magazine and the Creative Director for *1555* Magazine. His fiction and non-fiction pieces have been published in *The Isis* Magazine, *Industry* Magazine, *1555* Magazine, and *Common Ground* Magazine.

ANTONIA CUNDY is an American Literature MPhil student at Corpus Christi College, Cambridge. Her published and unpublished (poetry and prose) can be found at www.antoniacundy.com. She is intent on becoming a writer.

HARRIET DAVID is currently in her second year studying for a Creative Writing MSt at Somerville college, Oxford.

LUKE DAWES is a third year Ruskin School of Art student at St. Edmund Hall, Oxford. His work can be seen at www.lukedawes.com.

FREYA DOGGETT is a 1st year Modern & Medieval Languages student at Queens' College, Cambridge. Having completed an Art Foundation Diploma last year before coming to Cambridge, she hopes to eventually prioritise painting as a prevailing part of her future career. Further works can be found through contacting freyadoggett@hotmail.co.uk

SAM DUNNETT is a final year English Student at Wadham College, Oxford. Alongside poems and criticism for *The Oxford Review of Books* and *The ISIS* Magazine, he has composed a number of SMS messages for his friends and loved ones.

CHRISTY EDWALL is finishing a DPhil in English Literature at New College, Oxford. Her short stories have been published by Granta and The Stinging Fly.

EMILY FITZELL is a PhD student in literature and visual art at Trinity College, Cambridge. She has undertaken artist residencies to work on poetic / sculptural projects, and has twice been awarded the Powell Prize for serious verse. She is also a former editor of the *Mays*.

OMER FRIEDLANDER is a 3rd year English student at St Edmund's College, Cambridge. His work has appeared or is forthcoming in over a dozen publications in the UK, US, France, Israel and Canada.

ANJU GASTON is a finalist at Sidney Sussex College, Cambridge, where she studies Sociology. She is looking to work in the creative industries when she graduates and can be contacted at anjugaston@gmail.com.

JAMES GOLDING was born in West Yorkshire and grew up in the Ribble Valley, Lancashire. He is a final year medical student at Green Templeton College, Oxford.

MILLIE GUILLE is reading for the MSt in Creative Writing at Kellogg College, Oxford. She was longlisted for the 2017 National Poetry Competition, and runner-up in the 2017 Ambit Poetry Competition. You can find her on Twitter @MillieGuille.

AMADEUS HARTE is a masters student in Anthropology at St. Hugh's College Oxford. She previously studied Philosophy and Sociology at Trinity College Dublin whilst living in an anarchist squat. Her work is at www.remainunadapted1.wordpress.com.

ANNALISA HOADLEY is a Creative Writing postgraduate at Selwyn College, Cambridge. Winner of a coveted Blue Peter badge for poetry, two decades later she is working on her first manuscript, a blend of historical and future fiction. www.annalisahoadley.com.

SOPHIE HARDCASTLE is a Provost's Scholar at Worcester College, Oxford. She's an Australian published novelist and visual artist with a growing interest in poetry. Find more at www.sophiehardcastle.com

WILLIAM HOSIE reads English and French at Magdalen College, Oxford. He won first prize at the North London Festival of Music and Drama aged seven and has since declined a life of thespian glory in favour of mediocre poetry.

MINYING HUANG is a final-year Spanish and Arabic student at St John's College, Oxford. Her poetry has appeared in *PANK*, *Nat. Brut*, and *Electric Literature*, among others. You can find more of her work on Facebook @ minyinghuangpoetry.

JOY HUNTER is a second year Education and English student at Queens' College, Cambridge. Joy aspires to work in Film one day in a writing or directing capacity. Find more of her work at www.joyhunterwriting.wordpress.com

MARGARET 'LACEY' JONES is an Ertegun Scholar completing an MSt in Modern Theology at Lady Margaret Hall, Oxford. She writes fiction, essays, and poetry and will soon begin a PhD in English at Yale. See www.margaretlaceyjones.com for more.

ALANNAH LEWIS is a second year English student at Sidney Sussex college, Cambridge. An award-winning poet and screenwriter, her interests include discussing herself in third person, and scribbling. Results of the latter can be found at www.alannahlewisstories.wordpress.com.

CRYSTAL LIU is a 3rd-year Philosophy student at Worcester College, Oxford. She writes poetry and fiction.

WILL MACLEAN is a second year English student at Peterhouse, Cambridge from the West Midlands.

SUSAN MAGINN is a masters student of English literature at St. John's college, Oxford.

ELEANOR MYERSON is an MSt student in Medieval Literature at St Hilda's College, Oxford. She previously read English at Cambridge, where she received the T.R. Henn Prize for Original Composition. She is currently working on her first novel.

PAUL NORRIS is a 1st-year English student at Queens' College, Cambridge. He would like to write more, especially after university, and has more poems on www.thedefinitivearticle.wordpress.com.

PAIGE PINTO is an MPhil student in 18th Century and Romantic Studies at Lucy Cavendish College, Cambridge. She has previously been published in *In/Words*.

ROSHNI PRASAD is a postgraduate student at Peterhouse, Cambridge, and reads Strategy and Marketing at Judge Business School. She loves to write about university, travel and home; further works may be found at her blog, www.roshniwritesthings.tumblr.com.

ELAINE ROBERSTON is a finalist at the Ruskin School of Art Oxford. She is a curator, artist and comedian based in County Durham. Upcoming exhibitions, shows and projects can be found on her instagram @elainerobertson_

KATHERINE ROBINSON's poetry, fiction, and essays have appeared in *The Kenyon Review*, *The Hudson Review*, *Poetry Ireland*, *Poetry Wales*, *Ploughshares*, and elsewhere. She is doing a PhD in English at Pembroke College, Cambridge where she is writing a dissertation about Ted Hughes and The Mabinogi.

MATTHEW SECCOMBE is a 2nd-year Architect at Jesus College, Cambridge. He specialises in sketch drawings and paintings and has sold several pieces to art collections across the country. His artwork can be found on his website: www.etsy.com/uk/shop/MJSketch.

REBECCA SILLIS is a 3rd Year Law student at St John's College, Cambridge. Her preferred mediums are linocut and pen and ink. More examples of her work can be found at @becca_prints on Instagram.

WILLIAM SKELTON is in the first year of a MPhil in Cuneiform Studies at St. Benet's Hall, Oxford. He was published in the 2017 UCL Publisher's Prize Collection. He hopes to keep writing poetry and fiction after graduating.

SOPHIA SPRALJA is a visiting history of art student at Wadham College, Oxford. She worked for two years in New York under the fine art photographer Joel Sternfeld and fashion photographer Susanna Howe. Her website displays her photos: www.sophia-spralja-e8ry.squarespace.com

LUCY TILLER is a first-year English student at St Catharine's College, Cambridge. She is a Foyle Young Poet and a winner in First Story's National Writing Competition and was shortlisted in the Young Romantics Poetry Prize in 2017.

TIM TRAYHURN is a former electrician turned first-year English student at Wolfson College, Cambridge. He does not have any work available online; if you would like to see more please contact him directly at tbt23@cam.ac.uk

TOM WALDEN is a 2nd-year English student at Fitzwilliam College, Cambridge. He has a keen interest in journalism and poetry. His poems can be found on: www.tcwpoems.blog.

FLORENCE WARD is a 2nd-year English student at St. Catherine's College, Oxford. She was the editor of Isis Magazine in Michaelmas 2017 and has since then undertaken a number of roles in Cherwell, and hopes to pursue a career in journalism.

MARTHA WEST is a first year English student and keen actor at Balliol College, Oxford. She writes poems and spoken word in secret and has only just begun to dare try publish anything. She hopes to write plays and films in the future and act in them too.

GRACE WHORRALL-CAMPBELL is a 3rd year Historian at Newnham College, Cambridge. Before that she completed a Foundation Diploma in Fine Art at Central Saint Martins. She hopes to continue onto an MPhil in Modern British History next year, as well as to keep developing her art practice.

ALICE YU FREDERICK is pursuing an MPhil in Theoretical and Applied Linguistics at Lucy Cavendish College, Cambridge. She previously minored in creative writing as an undergraduate in the United States.